Business English in a Global Context

Best Practice
Upper Intermediate

Sarah Helm and Rebecca Utteridge

Teachers' Resource Book

Minnesota English Language Program

THOMSON

★

TM

HEINLE

United Kingdom • United States • Australia • Canada • Mexico • Singapore • Spain

THOMSON

---✶--- ™

HEINLE

Best Practice Upper Intermediate Teachers' Resource Book
Sara Helm / Rebecca Utteridge

Editorial Director: *Joe Dougherty*
VP, Director of Content Development: *Anita Raducanu*
Director of Product Marketing: *Amy Mabley*
Executive Editor: *Bryan Fletcher*
Development Editor: *Sarah O'Driscoll*
Production Editor: *Joan Ho*

Cover Image: *Getty Images*

Manufacturing Buyer: *Maeve Healy*
Compositor: *Oxford Designers & Illustrators*
Project Manager: *Howard Middle/HM ELT Services*
Text Designer: *Oxford Designers & Illustrators*
Cover Designer: *Thomas Manss & Company*
Printer: *Canale*

Printed in Italy.
1 2 3 4 5 6 7 8 9 10 ⁻ 11 10 09 08 07

For more information contact Thomson Learning, High Holborn House, 50/51 Bedford Row, London WC1R 4LR United Kingdom or Thomson Heinle, 25 Thomson Place, Boston, Massachusetts 02210 USA. You can visit our website at elt.heinle.com

ISBN: 978-1-4240-0068-5

Contents

	Coursebook contents	4
	Introduction	6
MODULE 1	PEOPLE	9
MODULE 2	MARKETS	39
MODULE 3	MONEY	69
MODULE 4	WRITING RESOURCE	99
	PHOTOCOPIABLE RESOURCE	103

Coursebook contents

Best Practice is a business English series designed for both pre-work and in-work students. Its topic-based modules train students in the skills needed to communicate in the professional and personal sides of modern business life.

MODULE 1 PEOPLE

This module explores the theme of people in business, through discussion of the advantages and disadvantages of different leadership styles, positive and negative leadership attributes and students' own experiences of ineffective leadership.

	Business Inputs	Language Work	Communication	Business across Cultures
1 Leadership	**Listening**: An interview about leadership styles **Reading**: Top Seven Leadership Mistakes	**Grammar**: Modals	Profiling your own communication style	International leadership
2 Dream teams	**Listening**: A conversation about problems within a team **Reading**: An article about a teambuilding session	**Expressions**: Idioms	Active listening	Understanding the team
3 Independence	**Listening**: Attitudes towards independent working **Reading**: Would you make a successful freelancer?	**Grammar**: Conditionals	Influencing	Motivation at work
4 Are you being served?	**Listening**: An interview about private and public sector services **Reading**: A report on customer service in the UK	**Grammar**: Relative clauses	Getting your message across	Organisational cultures

Business Scenario 1 Mediaco

Review and Development 1–4

MODULE 2 MARKETS

pages 34–63

This module examines the area of markets, exploring the issues relating to foreign markets, finding a unique selling proposition for your company, choosing the right brand strategy and how companies advertise to both niche and mass markets.

	Business Inputs	Language Work	Communication	Business across Cultures
5 Entering new markets	**Listening**: Different ways of getting into new markets **Reading**: Joint ventures in India	**Grammar**: Determiners and quantifiers	**Presentations**: Engaging your audience 1	India
6 The right look	**Reading**: Zara: The future of fast fashion	**Grammar**: The passive	**Presentations**: Engaging your audience 2	Dress
7 Brand strategy	**Reading**: Extending a brand **Listening**: Consumers compare local and global brands	**Grammar**: Making comparisons	Interviewing	Branding nations
8 The hard sell	**Reading**: Product placement in films **Listening**: An interview about reaching the Hispanic market in the US	**Grammar**: Making predictions	Feedback	Global marketing

Business Scenario 2 Dua

Review and Development 5–8

4

MODULE 3 MONEY

pages 64–93

The themes in this module reflect the subject of money, and include the discussion of emerging private sector markets, the pros and cons of investing in such markets, improving company finances, and getting third world countries out of the poverty trap.

		Business Inputs	Language Work	Communication	Business across Cultures
9	A thriving economy	**Reading**: An article about the private sector in China **Listening**: The growth of the Chinese economy	**Grammar**: Cause and effect	Leading meetings	China
10	Foreign investment	**Reading**: Foreign direct investment **Listening**: An interview with a country-risk analysis specialist	**Grammar**: Referring and sequencing	Participating in meetings	Russia
11	The bottom line	**Reading**: Tips on how to beat a recession **Listening**: Talking about budgets	**Grammar**: Prepositions	**Negotiations 1**: Bargaining	Brazil
12	Escaping poverty	**Reading**: Factors associated with poverty **Listening**: An interview about microfinance	**Grammar**: Reported speech	**Negotiations 2**: Handling conflict	Africa

Business Scenario 3 Katabaro Hotel

Review and Development 9–12

MODULE 4 WRITING RESOURCE

pages 94–99

13	Developing people	Advertisements, Emails
14	Local partners	Business reports
15	Getting away from it!	Press releases

Student B material	*pages 100–111*
Audio script	*pages 112–125*
Answer key	*pages 126–147*
Communication	*pages 148–150*
Business across Cultures	*pages 151–153*
Grammar overview	*pages 154–165*
Glossary	*pages 166–170*

Introduction

Best Practice Upper Intermediate is a four-level course designed for those learning English for international communication in business contexts.

It is suitable for:

- people working in companies and other organisations who use English for international communication
- pre-work students in business schools or further/higher education where business English is taught

Course components

- Coursebook
- This Teachers' Resource Book
- Workbook
- Audio cassette set / CD
- Testing and evaluation

Learning approach

The Coursebook consists of three main modules each comprising four units, with an additional range of built-in reference and resource sections. Both the Communication pages and the Business across Cultures pages stand alone and have their own clearly defined syllabus. Together, and combined with other course components, such as the Workbook, these elements provide great flexibility in course planning for varying periods of study and for learners with different needs.

Emphasis is on developing spoken **communication**, with mini role-plays, information gap activities and listening activities.

Writing is also well covered, with a section of seven units that further develop writing skills in business contexts.

Intercultural issues are an important feature of each unit and these are dealt with through the use of case studies, discussion activities, and listening tasks.

Unit structure

The Coursebook is designed to develop the four skills of **listening, speaking, reading** and **writing**. Each unit provides material for approximately three hours of classroom activity and combines a variety of these elements.

The **language syllabus** is based around:

Grammar. All the key structures for the level are covered. Grammatical structures are consolidated through communication activities.

Communication. The course covers key functional language for engaging your audience, interviewing, and leading meetings. There is also emphasis on 'social' English in business contexts, which is often requested by learners and teachers.

Vocabulary. A range of general and business areas is included. Key vocabulary areas for the level are presented. Emphasis is also put on word combinations.

These inputs are often contained in **reading texts, simulated web pages** or **listening extracts.**

Other important elements of the Coursebook units are:

Fact features. At the start of each unit, there is a fact feature, giving key snippets of information relating to the business area of the unit. These can be used to initiate discussion and prepare students for the theme of each unit.

Key language boxes. Each Communication section features a Key language box which introduces useful phrases related to the topic of the unit.

Business across Cultures. Each unit includes a section on an intercultural issue commonly faced by international business people. The aim of this section is to provide students with an awareness of intercultural terms and concepts in a clear and simple way.

Role-plays. A key element of *Best Practice Upper Intermediate* is the role-play sections. These sections give learners systematic opportunities to apply and use the language that they have seen in the Communication section. The sections where they do this have been chosen to mirror the ones they are likely to encounter in their own work situations.

Business Scenarios. After the four main units of each module, there is a Business Scenario unit, the aim of which is to consolidate the language and skills that are introduced in the module. It consists of a variety of activities all relating to one business situation, and its main feature is a communication activity such as a meeting or presentation. Finally, there is a writing task which relates to the content or outcome of the communication task.

Review and Development. Each module ends with a Review and Development unit which provides students with further practice of the grammar points, vocabulary and communication skills presented in the module.

Course outcomes

At the end of the course, learners will:

- be able to perform **practical business tasks** such as discussing their ideas and expressing their opinions, engaging their audience, giving a presentation and so on

- be used to hearing a **range of accents**, both native and non-native

- be able to use **business vocabulary** to speak and write about a range of business topics: leadership styles, market entry, budgets etc.

- be able to **apply their grammatical knowledge** to different professional and personal contexts, rather than treating grammar as an end in itself

- **have learned how to learn** – this is actively developed in the course, for example in learning grammar by discovery, and in developing vocabulary through typical word combinations to build larger blocks of language

- be aware of different values, behaviour and styles of communication in other cultures and, therefore, **operate more effectively in an international environment**

Overall organisation of the Coursebook

The subject matter has been designed to appeal to **adult learners in a business context**.

The core units are grouped into **three main modules**.

Module 1: People

This module looks at leadership, teamwork, independent working and satisfaction within the public and private sector – areas that both experienced and pre-work students can easily relate to.

Module 2: Markets

Here we examine the different forms of market entry, finding a unique selling proposition for your company, brand strategy and advertising to the mass and niche markets.

Module 3: Money

Learners look at a range of areas relating to money, such as emerging markets, foreign investment, improving company finances and getting developing countries out of debt.

Writing resource

In this module, students practise writing a number of realistic texts such as emails, business reports and press releases. This module also provides reading practice and some model examples of emails, business reports and press releases.

Further resources section

The final pages of the Coursebook contain:

Photocopiable resource. This section contains information and photocopiable material for pair and group work.

Audio script. All listening material is included.

Answer key. Answers to all the exercises are included.

Communication. This section corresponds to the Communication sections in the main units. It provides additional information on the language, as well as other issues such as body language, intercultural awareness, intonation etc.

Business across Cultures. This section provides further information on the issues that feature in each Business across Cultures section.

Grammar overview. This reference section includes all the main grammar points covered in the book. It allows learners to check that they have grasped all the grammar they need to know at this level. It reviews and expands on the key information presented in the book and also gives students the opportunity to practise it again through a variety of exercises.

Glossary. This section provides students with a detailed glossary of the key terms presented in the book.

For a full overview of the contents of the Coursebook, please see the contents list of your book. If short of time and unable to cover all the material, you can use it to select areas and activities of particular relevance to your learners.

The Workbook

The Workbook of *Best Practice Upper Intermediate* has been designed to fulfil several functions, and can be used as a logical and dynamic framework in which the Coursebook materials can be reinforced.

The Workbook themes follow those of the Coursebook, unit by unit. Many Workbook units contain **writing** exercises, most of which are ideal for homework.

There are basically two ways to exploit the Workbook: either at the end of each unit (the 'classic' method) or during the teaching of each unit as different grammatical/functional points arise. Use of the Workbook will vary depending on the unit.

The Workbook has been designed and written to be more than a 'homework depository'. It is down to the teacher to provide an impetus for its use, and through dynamic classroom practices, to show how the Coursebook and Workbook can form a 'learning synergy' for the benefit of students.

The audio materials

Listening materials are available on both CD and audio cassette. These feature the **listening** exercises presented in the Coursebook and present a range of accents, not only of people from different parts of the English-speaking world, but also a number of non-native accents.

This Teachers' Resource Book

A 'maximalist' approach has been adopted in this Teachers' Resource Book, which has been written with two potential 'teacher audiences' in mind: teachers who are relatively inexperienced in teaching professional English and require step-by-step guidelines, and more experienced teachers who might welcome some of the suggestions but ignore others.

This approach is clear from the layout of the Teachers' Resource Book:

Module overview. At the beginning of each module there is an overview which gives all necessary background information, including business and cultural notes.

Preview. At the beginning of each unit there is a short description of the grammar, functions and vocabulary to be encountered, pointing out grammar meanings and suggesting potential student difficulties.

Introductory activities. These are suggested at the beginning of each unit.

Step-by-step notes. The Teachers' Resource Book follows the Coursebook contents step-by-step, suggesting presentational, brainstorming and discussion activities as well as different ways of exploiting the audio component.

In many units, stress and intonation exercises are suggested, as well as grammar consolidation and vocabulary building tasks.

Answer keys follow each exercise where appropriate, and all audio scripts are presented in full as they occur throughout the units.

At the end of each unit, the **Checklist** usually suggests a final review activity of the main grammatical/functional elements of the unit.

Some general points

The exact number of audio plays is rarely indicated, as this depends on the listening level and motivation of the class – something best known to the teacher.

Normally, in the core units, it is not specified whether students do an exercise individually or in pairs, with pair checking or whole class feedback. Again, this is best left to the individual teacher.

During the role-play activities, it is important to go over the particular roles of Students A and B, checking that they understand the vocabulary and requirements of the role. It may be necessary to help with question formation prior to beginning the activity.

Do not hesitate to skip exercises if the class seems not to need them. On the other hand, do review ill-assimilated elements (without repeating the exercises, if possible).

If you have a long (i.e. extensive) course, aim to vary the exploitation as much as possible, using the Workbook as review and the role-plays, information exchanges, and grammar overview to a maximum. You could use simple or 'doctored' authentic materials as additional input; suggestions are included in the Teachers' Resource Book. If you have a short (i.e. intensive) course, concentrate on the main grammar points, the most important vocabulary and functional areas to link with the students' needs, and the maximum listening input.

Photocopiable resources. Each module includes three photocopiable activities, found on pages 103–120. These include communication activities such as role-plays or information exchanges suitable for pair or small-group exploitation in class. These activities have been designed to review/practise the main grammatical/functional features of

the different modules, adding a personal element where possible. Detailed exploitation suggestions for each activity are given (see pages 103–107).

Frameworks. There are seven frameworks, which can be found on pages 121–127, to be used before or after communication exercises. Some have been designed to help students prepare for communication tasks while others provide teachers with a clear structure for providing feedback. Appropriate stages at which to use specific frameworks are suggested in this Teachers' Resource Book.

Best Practice Upper Intermediate corresponds to BEC Vantage leading to BEC Higher by the end of the book, and CEF levels B2–C1.

We hope you and your students enjoy using *Best Practice Upper Intermediate* and its companion books at *Elementary*, *Pre-intermediate* and *Intermediate* levels.

People

MODULE OVERVIEW

AIMS AND OBJECTIVES

This module explores the theme of people in business, through discussion of the advantages and disadvantages of different leadership styles, positive and negative leadership attributes and students' own experiences of ineffective leadership. It develops the people theme into the topics of teamwork, self-employment and customer service, which both work-experienced and pre-work students can relate to easily. Throughout the units, a large vocabulary bank is built up and the use of noun combinations and verb / noun collocations are introduced for more advanced discussion of business topics. The grammar and functions practised in the module reflect elements of these themes: modals for talking about obligation, necessity and possibility at work, the conditionals for discussing many aspects of business, such as presenting facts and decision making, and relative clauses for business writing. The module's communication skills sections help students to develop a more advanced style of communication through skills such as active listening and influencing. The Business across Cultures sections in this module explore how leadership style can influence the culture of an organisation. They also examine differences between organisational cultures as well as cultural diversity within international teams. Students consider motivational needs and how they influence our behaviour.

At the end of the module, students should be able to:

- talk about obligations, necessity and possibility, using appropriate modals in their passive, past and continuous forms
- use the full range of conditionals to discuss aspects of their work
- use relative clauses more effectively in their written work
- discuss and compare leadership styles and characteristics
- talk about teamworking issues and qualities needed for effective teamwork
- assess the advantages and disadvantages of self-employment and their suitability for it
- use noun combinations and idiomatic phrases to talk about teambuilding
- use verb / noun collocations to discuss customer service in the public and private sectors and how to improve it

- achieve effective communication through checking, clarifying and confirming understanding and identify a variety of communication styles, including their own main style
- package their message clearly using appropriate phrases
- adapt their communication style to persuade and negotiate more effectively
- understand the impact of leadership style on organisations
- identify different personality types within international teams
- understand different motivational needs and how they influence our behaviour
- recognise the advantages and disadvantages of different organisational cultures

THEMATIC OVERVIEW

The themes in this module are interlinked through their association with the word, *people*. In business, *people* and the way they perform are the key to success. To achieve greater performance, companies strive to improve their leaders' and their employees' effectiveness. Companies are aware that both leaders and teams need to be developed constantly. If leaders 'inspire' and their teams 'gel', business productivity will improve and important areas such as customer service levels and customer satisfaction will improve. Effective communication is one of the areas which both the employed and the self-employed can improve in order to raise their level of performance. Learners with little or no experience in the world of work can easily relate to these themes which can often be translated into everyday experience, such as being part of a team or being led in a particular activity. Equally, any student will have opinions about customer service standards. Finally, whether to be employed or self-employed is a preoccupation for people about to enter the work market or seeking a change of career.

MAIN AUDIO CONTENTS

UNIT 1: interview in which a leadership specialist describes leadership characteristics and whether these only come naturally or can be developed; leadership styles and developing leadership competencies; extracts of different communication styles; extract featuring an independent financial consultant talking about the company cultures of two organisations she has worked for.

UNIT 2: dialogue in which managers talk about current teamworking difficulties and how to improve the team; dialogue demonstrating active listening techniques for clearer communication; extract in which members of a cross-border team introduce themselves at the start of a meeting.

UNIT 3: extracts in which self-employed people discuss the advantages and disadvantages of independent working; dialogues which demonstrate the push and pull approach to influencing others; extracts in which two people talk about their jobs in terms of company culture and management style; a businessman talks about his key relationships at work.

UNIT 4: interview about service levels in the public and private sectors; telephone conversation which demonstrates how to package your message for clearer communication; a job interview during which the organisational cultures of the candidate's current and possible new job are discussed.

PHOTOCOPIABLE RESOURCES (PAGES 108–111)

1.1 can be used any time after Unit 2.
1.2 can be used any time after Unit 3.
1.3 can be used after the Business across Cultures section of Unit 3.

BUSINESS AND CULTURAL NOTES

The *Business across Cultures* sections are intended to increase students' awareness of cultural as well as individual differences in leadership style and performance in cross-border and cross-functional teams. They also deal with the issue of 'cultural fit', a term used to describe the 'fit' between a job applicant or a merging partner company with another company's cultural values, expectations and attitudes. Students profile their own company culture, motivational needs, and personality and analyse different styles of management and corporate values.

1 Leadership

Vocabulary and listening
The vocabulary in this unit deals with positive and negative adjectives to describe leaders and their teams, such as *motivated* and *inspiring*. This vocabulary features in a listening exercise in which a leadership style specialist talks about different leadership styles and their advantages and disadvantages.

Reading and speaking
This section discusses leadership mistakes and gives students the opportunity to discuss their own experiences of ineffective leadership.

Grammar ## modals
Modals of necessity, obligation and possibility are presented in their passive, continuous and past forms.

communication ## profiling your own communication style
This section gets students to analyse their own communication style and decide which style they might like to develop further.

Business across Cultures ## international leadership
This section examines different leadership styles. Students describe the cultural profiles of various organisations, including their own, and consider ways in which leaders can maintain and encourage corporate values.

Introductory activity

With Coursebooks closed, explain that the unit theme is leadership. Elicit the names of a few famous living or dead political, business, military or sporting leaders. Write them up on the board. Ask students to describe to the class what type of activity they are / were famous for leading, in which country, etc.

Start-up

Ask students to turn to page 4 of their Coursebooks. Direct students' attention to the quotation about leadership at the top of the page. Ask pairs to discuss the leadership style of one or two famous political or business leaders on the board and report this back to the class briefly. Elicit adjectives to describe the leadership styles discussed by the students. Put a spidergram word field on the board and add the students' adjectives to it. Next, ask students to brainstorm a few specific types of

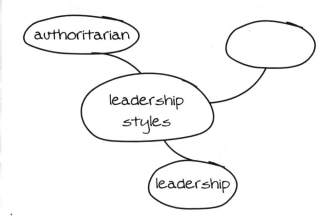

organisations they know of. Answers might include: *sports teams, clubs and societies, armies, private companies, state companies, charities, political parties, governments*. Ask pairs to discuss the questions in the start-up exercise, bearing these organisations in mind, and report their ideas to the class briefly.

Depending on your class, expand this into a class discussion about styles of leadership in specific types of organisation. Add any more useful vocabulary relating to *leadership styles* to the *leadership* word field.

Vocabulary and listening

A Ask students to work in pairs to do the exercise as indicated in the Coursebook. Do a class review of their ideas, using the organisations they brainstormed in the start-up exercise, to justify their answers. *Audaciousness* might be viewed as being a negative characteristic in the banking industry but a positive one in the fashion industry, for example. Add new vocabulary items relating to *leadership characteristics* to the *leadership* word field.

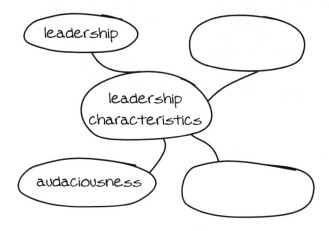

B Pre-teach vocabulary items such as: *bully, to surpass yourself, doormat, to get on with* (to have a good relationship with). Ask students to complete this exercise individually, before a class comprehension check. Add any new *leadership idioms* to the *leadership* word field.

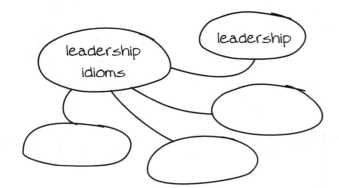

By the end of the unit the word field might be starting to look like the one below – with vocabulary of course! The same process can be followed in each of the Coursebook units.

Leadership should now be the central word bubble.

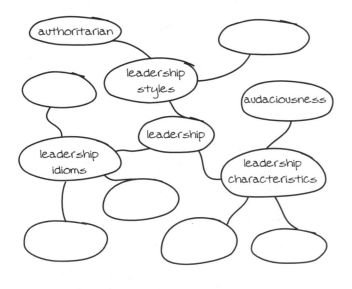

KEY

1 visionary	2 charismatic	3 intimidating
4 authoritarian	5 inspiring	6 subservient

C AUDIO **1.1** Explain that the class are going to listen to an interview with James Bartley, a specialist on leadership styles. Play the audio and do a quick class check of the leadership characteristics mentioned. Elicit synonyms for the following: *inborn, natural, innate,* and ask if the class agree with the idea that leadership can be learnt. Elicit examples of leaders to support their arguments.

KEY

1 charismatic   visionary   inspiring   audacious

2 People can learn how to become competent leaders.

AUDIO SCRIPT

Interviewer: What characteristics do people need to become good leaders?

James Bartley: Well, we've all come across leaders with charisma, that magnetic quality that attracts other people. These individuals are visionary – they have a strong set of ideas and a strategic vision about how things can be different in the future, and how things can be improved. And they're inspiring –

people listen to them and want to follow them. And they are often audacious – they do things that were previously thought very difficult or impossible.

Interviewer: But these charismatic individuals are few and far between. I mean, can all people become leaders?

James Bartley: You're right. Not all people are natural leaders. But yes, it is possible to take people who don't have these qualities and develop them into competent leaders.

D AUDIO **1.2** After a quick read through and comprehension check of the exercise questions, ask students to listen to the second part of the interview and answer questions individually. Do a second listening if necessary, during which students can note down as many useful vocabulary items, or difficult pronunciation blocks, for a quick class pronunciation exercise. Alternatively, write the following phrases up on the board. Elicit the word stress patterns and get the class to practise these items until confident.

Pronunciation blocks might include: *task-focused leadership, management by results, management by objectives, performance-related pay, action-centred leadership, motivational issues.*

KEY

1 Task-focused leadership, also known as management by results or management by objectives.

2 When both the organisation and individuals are clear about the tasks they have to achieve.

3 Using incentives like performance-related pay doesn't motivate people deep-down.

4 Action-centred leadership. It is better because it thinks about the individual in their social and team situation within the organisation.

5 Management is about organising the staff to make sure things get done, whereas leadership is about defining what there is to be done and inspiring people about why they should do it well.

AUDIO SCRIPT

Interviewer: So, how do you go about developing people into competent leaders?

James Bartley: Well, one approach is encouraging them to use a leadership style called task-focused leadership, also known as management by results or management by objectives.

Interviewer: Right.

James Bartley: With this leadership style, the organisation is clear about the tasks it has to achieve, and the individuals are clear about what they have to achieve. Organisations often use incentives like performance-related pay to promote high performance and to get motivated employees.

Interviewer: And are there any downsides to using this approach?

James Bartley: The main danger is that, although people are given an objective and they then work towards it, it doesn't actually connect to their inner motivations – so they're not really motivated deep down.

Interviewer: So how do you take care of these motivational issues?

James Bartley: Well, you need to move on from task-focused leadership and start treating people as individuals. This is where something called action-centred leadership comes in. With action-centred leadership leaders concentrate on the whole package: the task, the person, and the team or the group that the person is in.

Interviewer: Right, I see. But where does the strategic vision come in that you were talking about at the beginning?

James Bartley: Well, the big strategic question for both the organisation and leaders is where the tasks come from – how you decide in the first place what tasks your team is going to undertake. In fact, it might be described as the difference between leadership and management. Management is organising the staff and making sure everything is done. Leadership is about defining what there is to be done and then inspiring people about why they should do it.

Extension activity: Put students into pairs / small groups and get them to write short descriptions for the target language or useful expressions they noted down during the listening activity. Each team then reads out its descriptions in turn and points are awarded to the team who guesses the language item correctly.

Examples may include:

Strategic vision – this is the ability to understand which tasks are a priority and work out who would best do those tasks

E Read through the questions with the class. Ask students to make notes on an organisation they know. Encourage them to use the target vocabulary (including extra items they may have come up with during the extension activity in exercise D). Get students to work with a new partner. They should exchange information and report their partner's ideas back to the class. Do a board review of any useful language which emerges.

▶ VOCABULARY REVIEW AND DEVELOPMENT, PAGE 30 OF THE COURSEBOOK, CAN BE DONE AT THIS STAGE.

Reading and speaking

A Read the introduction. Review a few contexts where effective leadership is vital. Write them up on the board to help students (particularly work–inexperienced ones) relate to this exercise. Ask pairs to think of and briefly discuss a few examples of ineffective leadership relating to their ideas on the board and then explain them to the class. Write up useful language items on the board for students to copy down.

B Pre-teach vocabulary items such as: *productivity drag, immune, constructive criticism*, before starting this exercise. Ask students to read the text and answer the questions individually. After a comprehension check, ask the class to give specific examples from their experience which relate to the individual leadership errors in the exercise. This could also be expanded into a brainstorming and speaking exercise on what sort of problems can result from these specific leadership mistakes.

KEY

1e	2d	3g	4b	5f	6c	7a

C Ask students to complete this exercise individually, and do a class answer check. You could expand the answer session into a brainstorming activity on the types of *checks and balances* a company might put in place to ensure its leaders don't make the mistakes outlined in the article.

KEY

1 T

2 F *If a worker cares enough to share criticism, the least you can do is listen.*

3 F *Leaders shouldn't do every job themselves.*

4 T

5 F *Leaders should learn about time management and goal setting.*

6 T

D Ask the class to state whether they disagree with any of the leadership mistakes stated in the article, justifying their opinions. Elicit any others they can think of. As an extension activity, elicit ideas for effective leadership practice. Answers might include: *involve employees in decision-making and change-management, keep the workforce informed of likely changes in structure, encourage a culture of reward and praise for excellent work.*

E Ask students to form new sub-groups for this exercise. One person in the group should present and justify the group's final decision. Note each group's choices and reasons on the board for comparison. Finally, each group should agree / disagree with choices made by other groups, stating why. Depending on your class, you might like to allow some time for class debate.

▶ FOR FURTHER READING AND VOCABULARY PRACTICE RELATING TO THE TOPIC OF LEADERSHIP, DIRECT STUDENTS TO PAGE 4 OF THE WORKBOOK.

Grammar
Modals

Elicit as many modals as possible from the class and write them up on the board randomly. Allow *have to* and *need to*. Whilst not 'pure' modals, they perform a modal function, are commonly used, and appear in the reading text and following exercises.

A Ask students to read the instructions on page 6 and do the exercise. Elicit that modals are always followed by an infinitive. Ask students to read through the presented modal sentences in their passive, continuous and past forms. Elicit which sentence is an example of each form.

KEY

Use the article to check your answers.

B Ask students to complete this exercise individually, reviewing the tense form of the infinitive used in each sentence.

KEY

1 be trying / try   2 worry   3 be given   4 have known

C Instruct students to match a function in the box to sentences 1–7. This exercise could be done as a pairwork activity to make it interactive. At this point, you might find it useful to review the difference in function between the positive and negative forms of *have to, need to* and *must*, as they can cause confusion for the learner. *Don't have to* and *don't need to* or *needn't* express lack of necessity, whereas *mustn't* expresses strong negative obligation. Ask the class to read the instructions on question forms and elicit a few examples of question sentences containing the presented modals. Write them up on the board.

KEY

1 permission   2 deduction   3 past habits
4 lack of obligation   5 obligation   6 possibility
7 lack of ability

D Do a quick class check to review advice on being an effective leader and mistakes leaders make. Students should work in pairs and do the exercise as indicated in the Coursebook.

Give students a little time to write down prompt sentences for this exercise first. Audio or video recording could add an element of fun and aid review of the role plays and target language with students.

Extension activity: Assign one of the presented modal verbs to each pair and ask them to write a positive or negative sentence, about an organisation they know. Encourage them to use a variety of forms of the infinitive. Answers might include: *We have to work 35 hours per week, You can't be considered for the management team without a university degree.* Do a review of each sentence on the board. Repeat the exercise with questions sentences.

► FOR FURTHER INFORMATION ON MODALS, REFER STUDENTS TO GRAMMAR OVERVIEW, PAGE 154 OF THE COURSEBOOK.

► FOR SELF-STUDY EXERCISES ON MODALS, SEE PAGE 6 OF THE WORKBOOK.

► GRAMMAR REVIEW AND DEVELOPMENT, PAGE 31 OF THE COURSEBOOK, CAN BE DONE AT THIS STAGE.

Communication

Profiling your own communication style

With Coursebooks closed, ask students to think about their own most typical communication style for a few moments. This may take some considerable prompting, as it is an extremely personal subject, which they may not have given much thought before. Prompt them with questions like: *How do you think other people view you when you talk to them? What impression do you create? Do you use strong / direct language? Do you get straight to the point? Do you listen before you speak? Do you tend to talk about facts or feelings? Are you careful before giving an answer? Do you prefer formal / informal situations?* Depending on your class, you might find it useful to encourage students only to talk about themselves, rather than others in the class! A board word field of students' ideas could provide a useful basis for future exercises.

A Ask students to turn to page 7 of their Coursebooks and read the introduction. After reviewing the model answer, instruct students to listen to the audio and do the exercise as indicated in the Coursebook. Ask questions about features of these different styles. Answers might include: *A complex style involves long sentences, an emotional style uses words like 'feel' and strong adjectives like 'awful'.* Students might like to say at this point if their opinion of their own typical communication style has changed.

KEY

1b   2b   3b   4a   5a   6a   7b

AUDIO SCRIPT

1
I wonder if we could think about this. Maybe we could look at a number of options and see what we think.
2
It's important to be clear. The process must be validated by the control staff and then reviewed on a two-month basis.
3
Why don't we just take a break? Let me know when you're ready to get together again and we'll see how far we can get.
4
There are two points. First, we have to analyse the results and then we have to decide whether to invest or not.
5
What do you think you should do? Have you thought about any options?
6
A: *So, if I understand you correctly, you feel we should build up a bigger stake?*

B: *Yes, that's right. I mean it's going to be difficult to really have any impact on the market otherwise, don't you think?*

A: *I'm not sure I understand why you say that?*
7
I am afraid I can't say any more. It's a difficult issue and we need to weigh up the pros and cons.

B Ask students to work in pairs and do the exercise as instructed in the Coursebook. Do a class answer check.

KEY

1 complex   2 active listening   3 emotional
4 direct   5 giving advice   6 impersonal   7 formal

C After a comprehension run through of the scenarios, assign one to each group.

Remind each student to stick mainly to one style of communication. Appoint a pair to observe each group, in order to give feedback to the class on the styles they heard, with examples. An element of humour can be introduced if, in a second round of role plays, students adopt 'inappropriate' communication styles. This can also highlight the effect of a particular communication style on the listener. Audio or video recording the activity could aid a class review.

D Ask each student to consider their own dominant style, and whether they would find it useful to develop it in another direction. Get students to write a 'personal goals statement' about their communication style focus for the future. At regular intervals throughout the course, they could be given feedback on ways in which they have achieved this or suggestions for improvement.

Extension activity: To tie this lesson in with the unit theme of leadership, you could ask pairs to discuss the type(s) of communication style which an effective leader *should* exhibit, giving examples of leaders they know or have seen on television for example. Answers may vary, depending on the culture of your students, which could round off the unit theme with an interesting class discussion, involving key grammar and vocabulary items.

► FOR DEVELOPMENT AND CONSOLIDATION OF THE LANGUAGE ABOVE, SEE PAGE 7 OF THE WORKBOOK.

► REFER STUDENTS TO PAGE 148 OF THE COURSEBOOK FOR A SUMMARY OF THE POINTS COVERED IN THIS COMMUNICATION SECTION.

Business across Cultures
International leadership
Read the introduction together.

Leadership styles

A Read the instructions and check students' understanding of the words in the box. Students may not understand the meaning of *process-driven* (this type of organisation is bureaucratic and has strict procedures) and *personality-driven* (a good example is Microsoft with Bill Gates' own behaviour, working style, work ethics and so on influencing the whole of the organisation).

Play the audio and get students to compare their answers in pairs. Do a class answer check, asking students to give reasons for their answers.

KEY

Invesco Investment: *male-orientated   competitive personality-driven   results-orientated   hierarchical long hours*

Markhams Derivatives: *impersonal   fair managing results   process-driven*

AUDIO SCRIPT

Invesco Investment was unbelievable. Everything was so competitive. People competed about getting the most clients, about who earned the most. You even competed to see who the last person to leave the office was! And I'm not just talking about Monday to Friday. It was often the same at the weekend. The culture was very macho. There were hardly any women there. For us, it was alien, an alien world where, if you wanted to succeed, you had to play their game and compete on their terms. The senior partners were all men and they ran the firm like it was their own kingdom. They all had offices on the top floor – you know these beautiful oak-panelled offices with leather arm chairs. The problem was they were a long way from the reality of what was going on with the workers. The managers would organise these team-bonding events a few times a year. We would all go somewhere remote and climb a mountain or raft down a raging river. Their personalities were really suited to these things. They loved the competition between teams and individuals and they thrived on winning.

Of course, they'd say that this type of culture was enormously successful – bottom line results were always excellent and we were constantly reminded where Invesco was in the league of investment banks – never far from the top.

Markhams Derivatives was a very different experience. The managers who ran the Singapore office were professional managers, recruited for their ability to manage results and people. Of course, some were better than others, but I would say that, on the whole, they had built a very professional culture where people did their jobs to the best of their ability, whatever their background or gender.

There were a lot of processes which the managers monitored. For example, you had a performance review every six months where you discussed your progress with your boss. I used to sometimes think they were just going through the motions.

I'm not sure if they really believed in it. But these systems did mean that everybody felt the culture was quite fair – you know – treated people equally. Maybe it was lacking a bit of spark because that team spirit wasn't there, and the results were maybe not so spectacular. But, it was a solid, well-managed company and less based on personality.

B Ask students to do the exercise as indicated then get them to compare their answers in small groups. Finally, check answers in class, and ask: *Which company do you think she enjoyed working for? Why?*

KEY

Use the audio script to check your answers.

C Ask students to do this exercise in pairs. Stress that they should come up with other adjectives, as indicated. Allow 10 minutes to prepare the profile. You could ask them to do it in the form of a presentation. If so, review some basic presentation phrases beforehand. Ask students to present their profiles to the rest of the class or, if you have a large class, to small groups. Tell students to make a note of the different adjectives used to describe leadership styles and company culture in each presentation. At the end, ask which adjectives were used and write them on the board.

Do not clean the board.

D Ask students to do the exercise individually. Encourage them to use some of the adjectives on the board and from exercise A. Allow up to 10 minutes to prepare the profile (or set it as a homework exercise). When students present their profiles to their partner, instruct the listener to take notes and check and clarify details. Afterwards, get each student to give a very brief summary of what their partner told them.

Cultural fit

Tell students to refer to the heading and ask what they understand by 'cultural fit' (this is a term used when talking about whether or not a job applicant or a merging partner company shares your company's cultural values, expectations and attitudes).

If your class is pre-experience, they may be unfamiliar with the process of mergers and acquisitions (M&As). Therefore, before embarking on exercise E, elicit the meaning of 'merger and acquisition' then ask: *Why do you think some mergers and acquisitions fail?* Get students to discuss this in subgroups. Some possible responses:

Over-optimistic expectations of the acquirer.

Conflicts of interest.

Not conducting a proper assessment of price and financial risks (Due Diligence).

Culture clash between the two organisations.

Employees view the merger as a threat.

E Ask students to do the exercise in pairs. Make sure that they consider the question in terms of *cultural fit*. Some possible responses:

The acquirer imposes its culture on the other organisation.

Failure to keep employees informed, so stereotypes of the other organisation develop. The two cultures are kept apart initially which reinforces an 'us versus them' attitude.

Not building a transition team to manage the differences between the two cultures.

F Go through the instructions in class then get students to read the texts on their own. Get two students to describe each business in their own words in front of the whole class.

Next, get students to read the strategies in pairs then decide what advice they would give. Set a time limit then invite them to share their ideas in class, writing all new ideas on the board.

A variation of this exercise would be to ask students to prepare a presentation to Mays management. Beforehand, elicit what should be included. For example:

Introduction ➔ *background / why consultants were called in*

Main body ➔ *Potential problems / risks, solutions and advice*

Summary

Values and leadership

With books closed, draw an iceberg on the board (just the triangle and water line) and explain that some people think that culture is like an iceberg. Ask students if they can guess why (some aspects of it can be seen above the surface, while deep below are elements which are not visible to an observer). Write just two or three cultural elements on the illustration (see below) then elicit the rest.

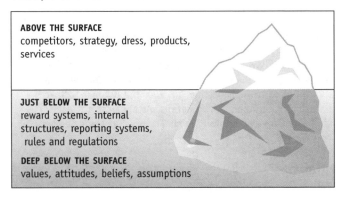

ABOVE THE SURFACE
competitors, strategy, dress, products, services

JUST BELOW THE SURFACE
reward systems, internal structures, reporting systems, rules and regulations

DEEP BELOW THE SURFACE
values, attitudes, beliefs, assumptions

G 1 Ask students to do the exercise as indicated in pairs. Check answers in class.

KEY			
Imaginative:	*creative*	*innovative*	
Hands-on:	*concrete*	*pragmatic*	*practical*
Professional:	*qualified*	*expert*	
Truthful:	*open*	*frank*	*honest*
Caring:	*supportive*	*nurturing*	

2 Students should discuss their ideas in pairs then compare them in class. Can the class agree on a definition for each value?

3 Get students to discuss their ideas in pairs then compare their ideas in class.

4 Ask students to discuss their ideas in small groups.

If their organisations do not have a written set of values, ask students to list the values that they think would suit their organisations and explain why they chose them.

▶ FOR A READING ACTIVITY ON LEADERSHIP STYLES IN DIFFERENT CULTURES SEE PAGE 8 OF THE WORKBOOK.

▶ REFER STUDENTS TO PAGE 151 OF THE COURSEBOOK FOR A SUMMARY OF THE POINTS COVERED IN THIS BUSINESS ACROSS CULTURES SECTION.

Checklist

Review the end of unit checklist items in the Coursebook with your students, as well as the unit word field. Add any interesting pronunciation items to the pronunciation file started in Unit 1.

As a final review of the main grammar and vocabulary items, ask pairs to write a statement about a specific leadership style, incorporating a modal verb practised in the grammar section. Explain that their statement should be false in their opinion, although grammatically correct. Get them to read it out to the class and ask the class to correct it to make a sentence they all agree with, changing either the modal verb or one or more of the vocabulary items. Allow students plenty of time for discussion and a variety of suggested answers, before they decide on their final statement.

Example sentence:

A charismatic leader must bully his or her team. Possible correction: A charismatic leader doesn't need to bully his or her team.

Extension activity: Word stress
This exercise is designed to revise students' understanding of primary word stress and introduce them to secondary word stress in longer words.

Write up the leadership adjectives from page 4. Alternatively, put the words on large cards so that they can be moved around the board, or the desk, for example.

Primary stress

Elicit that the primary stress falls on the following syllables:

charis**ma**tic   ins**pi**ring   **vi**sionary   authori**ta**rian

au**da**cious   in**ti**midating   sub**ser**vient   **mo**tivated

Pronunciation drill these words until all students are confident. Get the class to shout out each word in turn together, placing particular emphasis on the *most* stressed syllable. Elicit that it is pronounced in its full form. Elicit that to produce a stressed syllable, students are generally increasing their volume and raising their pitch.

Secondary stress

Once the students are confident at pronouncing these words, ask them to notice whether all of the other syllables are completely weak, or whether, in fact, in some of the words, students notice another, slightly stressed syllable:

charis**ma**tic   ins**pi**ring   **vi**sionary   au**tho**ri**ta**rian

au**da**cious   in**ti**mi**da**ting   sub**ser**vient   **mo**ti**va**ted

Students may notice that in the words with four or more syllables, another syllable is slightly stressed. Explain that this is a common feature of multi-syllable words, and is called secondary stress.

Pronunciation file O = primary stress **0** = secondary stress

o **O** o	o **0** oO oo	o **O** o o
inspiring	**authoritarian**	**intimidating**

audacious

Ask students to begin a key word pronunciation file. They should write down new vocabulary items, marking the correct primary and secondary stress above them, as in the example. Tell them to leave space underneath each word to collect other target vocabulary items with the same stress pattern, as they work through the units.

2   Dream teams

Vocabulary and speaking	This section presents language to talk about teamwork and teamworking skills, such as *time management* and *commitment*.
Listening and speaking	The subject of problem teams is discussed by Bob Fisher, a team leader, in an interview with Helen Clarke, a management consultant.
Reading and vocabulary	Expressions relating to teambuilding, such as *breaking the ice* and *breaking down barriers,* are presented in an article. Students discuss and present their opinions on the ideas in the article.
Vocabulary	Students learn and practise a range of business idioms in this section.
ommunication	**active listening** Students work on their active listening skills in order to increase the overall effectiveness of their communication.
usiness across Cultures	**understanding the team** This section looks at the importance of different personalities within teams. Students consider their own personality type and build a profile of themselves and a partner. They also role play a meeting in which they each assume a personality type.

Introductory activity

Find some magazine or Internet photos of teams working together in a variety of contexts if possible. Elicit what it is about the way the people in these photos are interacting that shows they are a team. Answers might include: *helping each other, open body language, eye contact, physical contact.*

Start-up

A Ask students to turn to page 10 of their Coursebooks. Direct students' attention to the statement about teams at the top of the page. Elicit the difference between *a great team of minds* and *a team of great minds* from the class. Ask students to vote on which they think is better for teams in business. Start a word field around the word *teamwork.* The category for this section should be *teamwork behaviour.*

Elicit a few different situations where teamwork is important, to provide a context. Answers might include: *sports teams, armies, company departments, sub-departments, projects, families, government departments.* With these teams in mind, ask small groups to discuss the question in this exercise, agree on a definition of a *'team'* and report their ideas to the class briefly. Allow some time for discussion about teams that students have experienced.

Vocabulary and speaking

A Ask students to do the exercise as indicated in the Coursebook, individually. As the two sets of sentences are opposites, there may not be much difficulty with new language items. Depending on your class, do a quick check of words such as: *preoccupied, innovative, tried and tested, upset.*

B Ask pairs to compare their answers to A and to agree on answers to B. Allow some time for discussion and personal examples, as pairs report their discussions back to the class. Add relevant phrases to your teamwork vocabulary word field.

C Pre-teach possibly difficult vocabulary items such as, *conflict avoidance,* before asking students to do this matching exercise individually.

KEY
1 *independence*
2 *commitment*
3 *communication*
4 *creativity*
5 *time management*
6 *conflict avoidance*
7 *performance*

D As the subject matter is potentially sensitive, depending on your class, leave this as an unreported pairwork exercise. Do a final review of all new vocabulary items with their pronunciation patterns and add them to your word field around the word *teamworking skills* or the pronunciation file started in Unit 1, where necessary.

Listening and speaking

A AUDIO **2.1** Explain that students are going to hear an interview between Bob Fisher, a team leader, and Helen Clarke, a management consultant, about some teamworking issues. After a quick read through of the questions, play the audio and do a class check of answers.

KEY

1

Nadine:	Conflict avoidance
Janet:	Independence
Karen:	Time management
Oliver:	Creativity
James:	Commitment

2 *Nadine and Oliver*

AUDIO SCRIPT

Helen Clarke: So, how've things been going with the team recently, Bob? I hear you've been having a few problems.

Bob Fisher: Yes, as you know, this was a new project, so we had to form a new team. Although some of the team members get on reasonably well together, the team as a whole seems a bit unmotivated. Some people work very hard and contribute a great deal but others are causing a few problems.

Helen Clarke: I see. Well let's look at each team member in turn and you can tell me what your main concerns are. How's Nadine getting on?

Bob Fisher: Nadine's a very important member of the team. She spends a lot of time listening to other team members and always provides them with the information they need. And she's very good at reducing friction and conflict between team members.

Helen Clarke: Well, no problem there. How about Janet?

Bob Fisher: Janet works very hard and she's always the first to arrive in the morning and the last to leave in the evening. My concern is that she just spends all day working on her own. In fact, she's a bit of a loner. She doesn't really understand that she needs to work as part of a team.

Helen Clarke: Umm. That's more worrying. She needs to realise how much you value working as part of a team just as much as individual performance. And Karen?

Bob Fisher: Karen's very enthusiastic but she's absolutely hopeless with time. She always seems to have last-minute panics when she has to get something done. This affects the rest of the team who've worked hard to meet their deadlines.

Helen Clarke: Oh dear. How about Oliver? I gather he's the least experienced of the team?

Bob Fisher: True, but what he lacks in experience he makes up for with new ideas. He's got a great imagination. He's very creative and he's a huge asset to the team.

Helen Clarke: Well that's good. And finally James. How about him?

Bob Fisher: At the start of the project he was very reliable and efficient. But recently, he seems to have lost interest and he's missed a few days off work.

Helen Clarke: Well, that needs to be addressed. Well Bob, I can see why you've been concerned. It sounds like you need to get them working together more – they need to gel as a team. Have you ever considered organising a team building course?

Bob Fisher: Well to be honest, no, but I ...

B Ask students to complete the exercise individually and play the audio again. Do a quick class check of answers. If necessary, do a third listening for students to note down as many useful vocabulary items, or difficult pronunciation blocks, for a class review.

KEY

1 get	2 friction	3 loner	4 panics
5 asset	6 gel		

C Ask pairs to role play this scenario. Get Student A to review the modals in the previous unit to help them give advice. Student B should focus on showing that they understand and appreciate Student A's advice, and ask further questions to check and clarify the situation.

Reading and vocabulary

A With Coursebooks closed, ask the class to give examples of teambuilding courses they have participated in or heard about. Answers might include: *outdoor adventure courses, snow or sand safari courses, mountain survival courses.* Elicit a few opinions about their usefulness. Encourage specific examples to personalise the context. Direct pairs to open their Coursebooks at page 11 and do the exercise together. Do a quick class review of their ideas, including ones the class have thought of. Write up useful vocabulary on the board.

B Direct the class to look at the article headline and elicit the type of teambuilding session it refers to. Ask questions such as: *What activities will take place? What sort of group would this be aimed at?* Ask students to read the article and then review the main ideas. At this point, tackle any vocabulary difficulties except for the expressions in italics.

C Instruct students to complete this exercise individually and do a quick class answer check.

KEY

1 *breaking down barriers*

2 *sceptical*

3 *engrossed in*

4 *get the pulse going*

5 *gimmick*

6 *whipping the group into a frenzy*

7 *breaking the ice*

D After a quick run through of the questions, ask small groups to discuss them and present their conclusions to the rest of the class. Get each group to present their answer to a different question. Invite comment and opinion from the other groups. Interesting ideas and language items should be added to the unit word field around the word *teambuilding*.

▶ FOR FURTHER READING AND VOCABULARY PRACTICE RELATING TO THE TOPIC OF TEAM WORK, DIRECT STUDENTS TO PAGE 9 OF THE WORKBOOK.

Vocabulary

A Explain that whilst this teambuilding activity is meant to be fun, there is a serious business aim behind it. Ask the class to suggest why the drumming company chose *Drumming up Business* as their name and what this idiomatic expression means? Possible answer: Try to find new business

B Run this as a pairwork exercise. Alternatively, you might like to make a set of 'verb' and 'expression' cards, distribute them round the class and get students to find their 'other half'. A review of the vocabulary and its literal meanings could be a useful memory device to help students relate to the idiomatic meanings.

KEY

1 pull	2 be	3 cut	4 think	5 face
6 pull	7 touch	8 take	9 have	10 go

C Ask pairs to match up the expression with its meaning. Again, this could be on a set of cards, distributed around the room.

KEY

1g	2f	3e	4a	5b
6j	7c	8i	9d	10h

D Instruct students to complete the text individually and do a class comprehension check.

KEY

1 touch base with you

2 pulls their weight

3 took on board

4 has a lot on her plate / is rushed off her feet

5 has gone through the roof

E Instruct pairs to do the exercise as in the Coursebook and do a class review.

▶ FOR SELF-STUDY EXERCISES ON IDIOMS, SEE PAGE 11 OF THE WORKBOOK.

▶ VOCABULARY REVIEW AND DEVELOPMENT, PAGE 31 OF THE COURSEBOOK, CAN BE DONE AT THIS STAGE.

▶ FOR LESS-CONTROLLED PRACTICE OF THE VOCABULARY IN UNITS 1 AND 2, REFER TO PHOTOCOPIABLE 1.1 ON PAGE 108.

Communication

Active listening

Direct the class to open their Coursebooks at page 13. Read through the opening statement with them. Ask pairs to discuss examples of people they know who are good listeners.

A AUDIO **2.2** Direct students' attention to the photo at the top of the page. Ask them to brainstorm a list of products it might be advertising. Answers might include: *lawnmower, lawn feed, swimming pool, lawn furniture*. After a read through of the two questions, play the audio and do a class answer check.

KEY

1 A lawnmower   2 By asking questions.

AUDIO SCRIPT

A: Hello Mr Blake, how are things?

B: Not too bad, thanks. In fact, we're off on holiday next week. We can't wait.

A: I'm sure. Where are you going?

B: We're trying Greece this year.

A: That should be lovely. Anyway, what can I do for you?

B: Well, we've been thinking about an upgrade.

A: OK, what sort of job do you have to do?

B: Well, it's pretty straightforward. Up and down. But it's a big area.

A: What are you currently using?

B: It's a rotary model. The Hayman 225. Not bad. But it's a bit slow.

A: Yes, you're right. In their day, they were one of the best, but there have been lots of improvements since then.

B: I agree. It's done very well but it's now probably time to trade it in.

A: So, you're looking for something a bit more powerful?

B: I think so. I wondered whether we might try a sit-on model.

A: That's certainly a possibility. Let me just make sure I've got the picture, you've got an area of ...?

B: I suppose around 300 square metres.

A: And fairly flat?

B: Yes, it's not too bad but ...

B Run through the key language in the box, and play the audio again. This exercise could be done as a pairwork exercise. Get pairs to read the active listening phrases with each other and do a round the class review to check pronunciation and intonation.

KEY

Use the audio script to check your answers.

C Get students to do the exercise as indicated in the Coursebook. At the end of this exercise, ask one or two pairs to perform in front of the group. During this open class role play appoint several observers for each one, to note down and give feedback on the active listening phrases the class heard, during a final class board review.

D Divide the class into small groups and assign discussion topics to each one. Again, getting an outside observer to note down and comment on each group's use of active listening techniques can help students to become more actively aware of their checking and clarifying techniques. Alternatively, video or audio record extracts from their discussions. Do a final review of the use of the target language.

Extension activity: Get the class to think about or invent a time they ran into an old friend on the street. Ask students to describe the content of the conversation in more detail, to build up a brief conversation scenario. Write up the different topics on the left hand side of the board to act as a reminder. Next, write up the category headings of active listening phrases from the key language box on the right hand side of the board. Then, thinking about the conversations described, get the class to brainstorm a few alternative active listening phrases they might use in the same way as the presented language items. Expand the categories if necessary. For example, *showing interest* could also be *showing surprise or disbelief*. Prompt students with questions such as: *What did you ask when he told you that ...? What was your reaction to that?* Open questions might start with a different question word, *which, when, why, how*, etc. Clarifying questions would follow suit. Other confirming comments might include: *Absolutely! I can see what you mean.* Write up (corrected) elicited phrases under their category headings. Get pairs to choose one or more of the elicited conversation topics. Ask them to do a short role play based on these conversations, using the newly elicited active listening phrases. Circulate collecting good examples of these. Get one or two pairs to role play their conversations in front of the class and ask the class to note down and give feedback on the phrases used. Give students time to write down all new active listening phrases.

▶ FOR DEVELOPMENT AND CONSOLIDATION OF THE LANGUAGE ABOVE, SEE PAGE 12 OF THE WORKBOOK.

▶ REFER STUDENTS TO PAGE 148 OF THE COURSEBOOK FOR A SUMMARY OF THE POINTS COVERED IN THIS COMMUNICATION SECTION.

Business across Cultures

Understanding the team

Ask students to keep their books closed. Draw a very simple sketch of a layered cake on the board, showing the cream in the middle, the layers of sponge, a thick base and icing on the top. First of all, explain that interculturalists are very fond of metaphors. Do the students remember the iceberg in Unit 1? Can they remember what it represented? According to Fredrik Fogelberg, a well-known management consultant, a layered cake is a good metaphor for an international team, which he believes is more than just a combination of national cultures. Tell students that the base of the cake represents the team's 'common purpose'. Instruct them to work in small groups and work out what the rest of the cake consists of. They can draw the cake and label it or simply brainstorm words on flipchart paper. It is no problem if they come up with completely different ideas from Fogelberg's; it will be interesting to compare them. Set a time limit and then get each group to share its ideas with the rest of the class. Finally, reveal the elements that Fogelberg included in his metaphor. Ask the students what they think of his metaphor. Can they think of a better one? Some people compare the different layers of culture with an 'onion'. (See Business across Cultures notes on page 151.)

See the following website for further information about Fogelberg's 'Napoleon' cake theory:
http://www.nomadiclife.nl/media/napoleoncake.pdf

Ⓐ Students should do the exercise in pairs as indicated in the Coursebook then compare their answers in class.

KEY

1d 2a 3e 4c 5b

Ⓑ Ask students to do the exercise in pairs then compare their answers in class.

You could also ask them if they can think of any other traits (positive or negative) belonging to each personality type.

Possible responses:

Controller –	Enjoys detailed work / Concentrates on one task for a long time
Seller –	Outgoing / Good at drumming up enthusiasm for new ideas
Negotiator –	Collaborative / Tends to listen / Shows empathy
Organiser –	Task-oriented / Working relationships tend to be business-like
Creator –	May develop systems and procedures that contradict the existing way of doing things / Thinks outside the box

KEY

1b 2e 3d 4c 5a

Ⓒ Match students with someone they don't work with very often and ask them to build a full profile of their partner by interviewing him / her. Tell them to imagine that their partner is a new member of their team and that they must introduce him / her to the other team members (i.e. the rest of the class or sub-group).

Students could build their own profile for homework.

Ⓓ AUDIO **2.3** Read the instructions together in class. Check understanding of *cross-functional* and *cross-border*. Draw students' attention to the team wheel, which they have to complete while listening, and tell them that they will hear five speakers. Play the audio once then check answers in class.

KEY

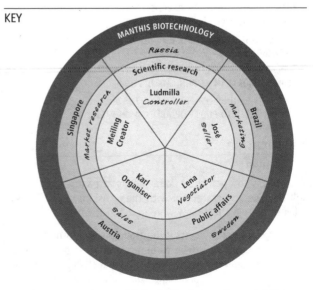

A: *Hi everyone. My name's Ludmilla Dementieva and I've been with Manthis for just a few months. I have a strong background in the sciences and I worked at the*

*Government Bioscience Laboratories in Russia, where I'm
from, for many years. Here, I've been appointed
Scientific Director and will be in charge of anti-viral
products. My job is to make sure that everything works
well and that we respect quality standards at all times.*

B: *Hello everybody. My name is José Borges and
I'm from Brazil. I've worked here for three
years and for the past six months I have
worked as Marketing Vice-President for Brazil. I
guess I'm the sort of guy who likes to promote
new ideas and products. I've always been on
the commercial side and I think we have a
great opportunity with this vaccine. So I'm
really looking forward to working with you all.*

C: *Good morning everyone. I think most of you know me.
For those of you who don't, my name's Lena Malmstrom
and I'm in charge of Public Affairs at a corporate level.
In my job, a lot of my time is spent working with people
in the biotechnology field. I have to ensure we are in
line with current legislation and public opinion. I'm
originally from Sweden but I've been based in our head
office here in Vienna for the last two years. In my
opinion, the success of these projects is always related to
the people. I like working in teams and I'm sure we can
build a really strong team here. I think the launch
strategy will be crucial to success of this product and
therefore for our company.*

D: *I'm Karl Berger. I also work here in the head office,
although I'm originally from Salzburg which is in the
north of Austria. I'm responsible for European Sales, so I
look after the distribution and sales of all our range of
products in Europe – that really means France, Germany,
Scandinavia, and of course, Austria. It's the sort of job
that requires tight schedules and very clear processes! I
think this launch is going to be a great opportunity for
Manthis but also a big challenge.*

E: *My name is Chen Meiling. I'm from Singapore. I work in
our regional office there and I am responsible for market
research in the South East Asian region. My job involves
not only researching the market but also coming up with
new approaches. As you probably know, Manthis has
targeted our region as having great sales potential and
this vaccine could really establish us in the market. This
is my first trip to Europe and I'm looking forward to
working with you on this project.*

Note that in Singapore, people who have Chinese names
usually introduce themselves by saying their surname first,
followed by their first name.

E Go through the instructions together. Tell students that
once they have done the matching exercise with a partner
you will play the audio again so they can check their
answers. Do a class answer check.

KEY

1b   2d   3c   4e   5a

F Get a different student to read each profile out loud in
class. Check understanding as you go along. Tell students to
discuss their ideas in pairs then compare them in class.

Possible responses are as follows:

Clashes may occur between ...

*... Russia and Singapore or Austria because of the lack of
rules in Russia.*

*... Brazil and Singapore or Austria because Brazilian
flexibility could be seen as stemming from a lack of formal
procedure.*

G Ask students to discuss these questions in subgroups. They
should then share their ideas with the rest of the class.

A typical response is as follows:

*They need a team leader to promote the identity of the
team, develop relations and agree on practices. Lena
Malmstrom should be the team leader due to her Swedish
consensus building and compromise.*

H Read the instructions together and divide the class into
groups of five. If the class is very small or you have an
uneven number, roles can be omitted. Assign a role to each
student and ensure that they do not disclose any details
about their role to the rest of their team. Once students
have read their roles, remind them that the aim of the
exercise is to work out which role each member of the team
is playing. You could write the following roles on the board
to focus their attention:

controller   seller   negotiator
organiser   creator

Allow approximately 10 minutes for the actual meeting.
Afterwards, ask students to write down who they thought
was playing which role on a piece of paper then discuss
their conclusions with their team.

▶ FOR FURTHER INFORMATION ON MULTICULTURAL TEAMS SEE PAGE 13
OF THE WORKBOOK.

▶ REFER STUDENTS TO PAGE 151 OF THE COURSEBOOK FOR A SUMMARY
OF THE POINTS COVERED IN THIS BUSINESS ACROSS CULTURES
SECTION.

Checklist

Review the end of unit checklist items in the Coursebook with
your students, as well as the unit word field. Add any
interesting pronunciation items to the pronunciation file started
in Unit 1.

Extension activities: Refer the class back to the first two unit
sections on teamworking skills. Ask students to write a very
short article about how they see their own teamworking
strengths and weaknesses and which aspects they would like to
improve on for the future. This could be a homework exercise,
which each student could read out in class after individual
correction and review.

Alternatively, review the reading exercise on teambuilding
events with the class and ask pairs to dream up their ideal
teambuilding event. They should include some of the idiomatic
phrases presented in the vocabulary section. Get them to
prepare a short presentation on their event to be made to the
class. After all the presentations have been made, get the class
to hold a meeting to discuss each event idea (in small groups)
and select the event they would like to hold for their (fictitious)
company.

Extension activity: Intonation patterns

Whilst linguists still disagree about how English intonation
works, they do agree that it is extremely important as it
communicates something about the speaker's attitude. Active
listening involves a considerable amount of intonation.

Ask students to look at Audio 2.2 again. Quickly elicit the active
listening phrases such as:

I'm sure, That should be lovely, Yes, you're right, I agree, So, you're looking for something a bit more powerful?'

Write them up on the board.

Before playing Audio 2.2 again, ask the class to listen for these points:

How does the listener indicate that they want to check or clarify a point? Example: *So, (rising pitch), pause before asking the question.*

Alternatively there may be a show of interest or understanding. Ask students what happens to the active listener's pitch and volume? *They generally go up.* Model the first confirmation phrase *I'm sure* with the correct intonation pattern. Elicit that pitch and volume rise to indicate understanding and agreement and mark a rising arrow over *sure*. Tell students they are going to listen to Audio 2.2 again and that they should mark pauses, rises and falls in intonation and volume above the active listening phrases in their script. Get students to do this individually and compare their answers with a partner. Do a class answer check, marking intonation patterns onto your board sentences.

Elicit that pitch generally rises at the end of a question and the voice also often gets louder for confirming comments, if the listener is being sincere. Interruption with a short 'So,' followed by a pause before the clarifying question, can add emphasis, and is important because it gives the person who was speaking time to get used to the idea of being interrupted with a question, which is more polite and less aggressive than simply interrupting with the question. Ask one or two pairs to act out the script to practise correct intonation patterns.

To add an element of humour and to highlight the negative effect of incorrect intonation patterns, get one pair to act out the script with completely flat intonation.

If you recorded your students' discussions in the previous communication activity in this unit, review one or two of their extracts again, so that students can analyse their own active listening intonation patterns.

3 Independence

Listening and speaking	The subject of working independently is discussed in a series of interviews with self-employed people. Students identify the advantages and disadvantages of this type of work.
Reading and speaking	Vocabulary relating to the personal qualities needed to be a successful freelancer, such as *independent* and *self-disciplined* is introduced in this section. Students decide whether or not they would make a good freelancer.
Grammar	**conditionals** Students study the main conditional forms: zero, first, second and third, in a variety of activities.
Communication	**influencing** The push and pull approach to negotiating is dealt with in this section.
Business across Cultures	**motivation at work** This section focuses on three motivational needs that work must satisfy: power, achievement, and affiliation. Students identify their own motivational needs and discuss what drives them.

Introductory activity

With Coursebooks closed, write the word *Independence* up on the board. Explain that it is the unit theme. Ask pairs to come up with a statement to describe what this word means to them. Elicit ideas from the class and allow the class time for questions and discussion about each statement if necessary. Write up any useful language on the board.

Start-up

Ask students to turn to page 16 of their Coursebooks. Direct students' attention to the photos. Elicit that the photos show people who are freelancers.

A Ask the class whether they, or their friends and relatives, have ever been self-employed and elicit a few typical types of self-employed work. Answers might include: *artists, writers, skilled trades workers, cleaners, IT specialists, graphic designers, finance advisers.*

B Ask students to estimate the percentage of self-employed people in their country, Europe and the US. Direct students' attention to the statistics about self-employment at the top of the page and find out which students had the closest answers. Find out how many of your class would find this an attractive way to earn a living.

C Elicit the sort of activities which are commonly outsourced by companies. Answers might include, *HR payroll and admin, IT services, cleaning, PR, design, accounting services.* Divide the class into two halves. Ask one half of the class to brainstorm benefits to companies, and the other to discuss potential downsides. Answers might include: *project benefits: outside expertise, lower overheads, short-term project downsides: communication problems, escalating costs.* During a class review, allow time for discussion and accounts of personal experience.

Listening and speaking

A Ask pairs to discuss the advantages and disadvantages of being self-employed or working from home and report their discussions back to the group. Answers might include, *comfortable surroundings, more flexible timetable / lack of structured work environment, easy to be distracted.*

As a review of these vocabulary items, as well as vocabulary introduced in the start-up discussions, create a word field around the subject of 'self-employment' on the board. Some of the categories in the word field below relate to later exercises in this unit.

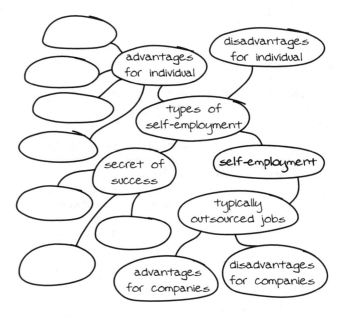

B AUDIO **3.1** Explain that students are going to hear four people talking about their attitudes to independent working. Ask them to complete the table. Play the audio and do a class answer check. Add key vocabulary to the unit word field, around the phrase, *secret of success*, for example.

KEY

	Freelance job	Training	Main advantage	Main disadvantage	Secret of success
1	Writer of children's books	None	Flexibility	Irregular and unpredictable income	Self-discipline
2	Independent Financial Adviser	Two-week training course	Independence	Income relies on how the economy is doing	Word of mouth and recommendations
3	IT Specialist	Degree	Variety	Investment	Keep in touch with clients and patience
4	Plumber	Technical college	Money	Difficult customers	Accurate estimates

AUDIO SCRIPT

1

I used to be a journalist, but when I had children I discovered I was good at telling stories, as my children really enjoyed them. So I decided to become a children's book writer. I suppose I have a natural talent as I didn't follow any particular training. You never know what's going to sell and what isn't, so my income is very irregular and unpredictable. I would say that's the main downside to being a writer. But the biggest advantage is the flexibility. I can use my time as I want. I would never go back to being a salaried employee, even if I was offered double my current income! I think my success comes from self-discipline – using time efficiently is certainly an issue for some people. I sit down every morning at 9 a.m. and I don't stop until I've written a thousand words. If I carry on being motivated and inspired, I'll continue to write a book a year.

2

In my last job I was a manager in a call centre, but four years ago I was made redundant. If I hadn't lost my job, I'd still be there. As I was already 56, I didn't think I had much chance of finding work in another company, so I decided to retrain as an independent financial adviser. I went on a two-week training course and now I visit people in their homes selling them financial products such as life insurance. I like the independence this gives me. The secret of success? Word of mouth – I find new clients through personal recommendations from existing clients, so I must be doing something right! Any disadvantages? Well, when the economy is doing badly, people cut back on buying financial products, and my income goes down. And then there's the problem of dealing with your admin and paperwork, but I'm reasonably organised about that.

3

I'm an IT specialist. I design computer systems for large engineering companies. I went freelance about seven years ago – I'd done a degree in computer science at university and I'd worked in an IT services company for twenty years but then I decided to strike out on my own. It was quite difficult in the beginning. I had to do a lot of networking and make a lot of contacts. This is still the most difficult part of my job. But if you want to succeed, you have to keep in touch with potential clients – and be patient because they may eventually offer you a contract! I guess the main disadvantage is the investment. You have to spend a lot of your own money on equipment, which you're always having to update. But it's worth it because of the variety that this kind of work offers – no two projects are the same.

4

I'm a plumber. I trained in a technical college after I left school at 16. My dad was a plumber and I didn't want to do anything else. Like him, I've always been self-employed. The worst thing about my job is that customers can be very difficult to deal with – they're always changing their minds. The best thing is the money. Plumbers have a reputation for earning a lot of money, and some of them do. I do quite well. I have a house in Spain, for example. My brother became a teacher, and I'm earning more than him. Of course, one issue is that you have to keep on top of your finances and your tax situation – it's crucial to get a decent accountant. The key to success is doing an accurate estimate for each job, and sticking to it – customers get very annoyed if it ends up costing more than you estimated at the beginning.

C Using the subject prompts, elicit a few questions that students would like to ask each other and write them up on the board. Get students to think of a few more questions to ask their partner. They should then interview their partner and report their partner's answers back to the class. Alternatively, run this as a mingling and networking exercise, with the class collectively reconstructing each student's profile in a class review afterwards.

D Ask pairs to do this exercise, as instructed in the Coursebook. Alternatively, write each category as a heading on different pieces of flipchart paper. Allow the class to mingle, asking each other questions and writing down useful and relevant phrases from their answers on the appropriate flipchart, which should be added to their unit word fields.

▶ FOR VOCABULARY PRACTICE RELATING TO THE TOPIC OF INDEPENDENCE, DIRECT STUDENTS TO PAGE 14 OF THE WORKBOOK.

▶ FOR LESS CONTROLLED PRACTICE OF THE VOCABULARY COVERED IN UNITS 1–3, SEE PHOTOCOPIABLE MATERIAL 1.1, PAGE 108.

Reading and speaking

A Students shouldn't have too much difficulty with the key vocabulary in this exercise, but depending on your class, pre-check items such as, *cash flow crisis, chase the debt, turn down work.*

B Ask students to do this exercise as indicated in the Coursebook before finding out the results on page 128 of the Coursebook. Ask pairs to discuss the results and report back to the class on why their partner feels they would or wouldn't make an ideal freelancer.

KEY

1a Never let clients think that you have cash flow problems. There is also a risk that the word will spread. Clients can cost you a great deal of time and money by not paying their debts so make sure you have a good system in place to manage this aspect of your business. Try to do a credit check to find out about the financial status and reliability of a potential customer.

2b Agencies often have a clause in their contracts which would prevent you from approaching the customer for new work in the future.

3b If you have a reliable, experienced and capable team, delegate as much as possible. You can't do everything! Working every weekend will only lead to burn-out.

4a Always act in the best interests of your clients. You will gain a reputation for honesty, integrity and professionalism.

5a Gain confidence by meeting a few people who also arrive early before it gets crowded.

6b In the long term, you cannot compete on price alone. Market (and gain a reputation for) your quality, service and value for money. However, consider reducing your rates for clients who have a limited budget but are likely to require ongoing work.

Score

5–6 → *You may have the ability to set up your own business. Nonetheless, do not give up your job until you are sure that there is a market for your skills as a freelancer.*
0–4 → *Do not rush to leave your job – It might be risky! Remember that working for someone else has its benefits ...*

C Ask small groups to review the units covered so far and prepare a list of suitable adjectives to describe the qualities needed to be a successful freelancer. They can then move round the class, comparing their lists with those of other groups. Possible answers: *flexible, organised, reliable, trustworthy, punctual, confident, energetic, driven, decisive, patient, motivated.* This category could be added to the word field started earlier in the unit. Add any difficult pronunciation items to the pronunciation file started in Unit 1.

D Ask pairs to read the email on page 100 of the Coursebook and jointly prepare a short presentation on 'Going Freelance'. Limit visuals to maximum three slides / flipchart pages, and set a short time limit of around 5 minutes per presentation. Audio or video recording these presentations would aid review of their strengths and weaknesses. Other students should be encouraged to ask questions, during or after each presentation.

▶ FOR FURTHER READING PRACTICE RELATING TO THE TOPIC OF INDEPENDENCE, DIRECT STUDENTS TO PAGE 15 OF THE WORKBOOK.

Grammar
Conditionals

A Ask the class to look at the sentences and match them to a heading in the box individually. Do a quick class answer check.

KEY

1 something that didn't actually happen

2 an imagined or hypothetical situation

3 something that you usually do

4 a possible event in the future

B As an open class exercise, get the class to match the sentences 1–4 in A with a conditional type: zero, first, second or third. Do a quick check and review the tense forms used in either part of each sentence.

KEY

1 third   2 second   3 zero   4 first

C Ask the class to do the exercise as instructed in the Coursebook individually. Do a class answer check.

KEY

1 look   2 will steal   3 would be
4 would have started   5 am offered

D Ask students to do the exercise in pairs. Do a quick class answer check.

KEY

1 fact

2 strong recommendation

3 prediction

4 past regret

5 unreal future situation

E Run through the model question with the class and get one or two students to answer it using the second conditional. As they are giving an answer, ask other questions to obtain more detailed information, using the conditionals, such as: *What would you do if a customer refused to pay you? What would you do if your business failed? What would you do if your business made you a multi-millionaire?* Ask pairs to ask each other and answer the next four questions in the same way. Encourage the questioner to ask further questions to expand the conversation in the same way as you modelled. Then get several students to repeat their partner's answers to the class, and get the class to note down and give feedback on the conditionals used. They should note the sentence and say which type of conditional was used and why. Example: *If I found a job abroad, I would have to get my sister to look after my dog. Conditional type: Conditional 2 with a phrasal modal. The speaker is describing a hypothetical or imagined (unreal) future.*

Extension activity: Ask the class to brainstorm five more conditional questions they could ask each other, relating to the past, present or future. Write each question up on the board. Ask the class to copy them down. Ask students to write a short one or two-sentence answer to each question on a clean sheet of paper. Ask them to space their answers out so that they can be cut up into strips at a later stage. The answers could be done as a homework exercise. Take in the sheets of paper and do individual correction with each student. Cut the sheets into strips so that each answer is on a separate strip. Read out a question followed by each student's answer. Award each strip of paper to the student who first guesses the identity of the person who wrote the answer. If appropriate, ask them to give their reasons – using conditionals where they can. Continue the process until you have distributed all the answer strips. The winner is the student who collects the most strips of paper.

▶ FOR FURTHER INFORMATION ON CONDITIONALS, REFER STUDENTS TO GRAMMAR OVERVIEW, PAGE 155 OF THE COURSEBOOK.

▶ FOR SELF-STUDY EXERCISES ON CONDITIONALS, SEE PAGE 16 OF THE WORKBOOK.

▶ GRAMMAR REVIEW AND DEVELOPMENT, PAGE 31 OF THE COURSEBOOK, CAN BE DONE AT THIS STAGE.

▶ PHOTOCOPIABLE 1.2, PAGE 109, CAN BE DONE AT THIS STAGE.

Communication

Influencing

Elicit one or two examples of situations in which students have tried to negotiate with others to influence an outcome. Emphasise that these need not necessarily be business situations. Students should describe their communicative strategy. Ask: *What type of language did they use? Did they take a direct / indirect approach? Were they successful?* Write up relevant ideas and vocabulary. Direct the class to open their Coursebooks at page 19 and read the statement on the *push* and *pull* approaches. Get students to decide whether the examples they gave described the *push* or *pull* approach.

Ⓐ Ask the class to read the two texts and do a quick comprehension check of vocabulary if necessary.

Ⓑ AUDIO **3.2** Direct the class to read through the Key language box. Elicit that the push approach is more direct than the pull approach. Read the two questions and do the exercise.

KEY

	Katja	Phil
1	Her manager	Client
2	Push	Pull

AUDIO SCRIPT

1

A: Have you got a minute?

B: Sure. Go ahead.

A: You remember we talked about my role during my last review?

B: Aha.

A: As I said then, when I joined BLK I understood my role was going to be in property assessment and surveying.

B: Yes, I explained ...

A: I know, but I wanted to make two points about my role. Firstly, my qualifications are in surveying and I think I am being wasted in my current role. Secondly, I wondered whether we could review our current working practice. I mean, a surveyor goes out and meets the vendor or agent and then views the property. He then passes on a file to me and I write a report. I don't mind writing the report but I could do it all. I have good contacts in the area and I'd like to be more 'out there' meeting the agents. It's important that we get to hear of opportunities as soon as possible. I could keep my ears open and build up good relationships with the agents. Then, as I said, I could also do some of the survey work. My training has prepared this for me so ...

B: Excuse me, Katja. But I guess this means you want more money!

2

A: Sally, just before we finish, can we take a look at the terms for next year?

B: I suppose so. Don't tell me. You want to put your prices up?

A: Well, could we start with our service?

B: Of course. As you know, we're very happy. The customer-facing training in particular has made a significant difference.

A: That's good news, and we can see the progress as well. I don't know if you have done any benchmarking on your competitors in this area?

B: Well, benchmarking is an ongoing process of ours. We think we're improving.

A: I'm sure you are. And we're pleased to be part of that. It seems to be a good change from just selling on price.

B: Absolutely, that's our strategy and I can see where you're going! So when did we last review your prices?

A: It was more than two years ago.

Ⓒ Play the audio again and ask the class to do the exercise as indicated in the Coursebook. During the class comprehension check, elicit that the speaker uses the *push* approach in the first example and the *pull* approach in the second one. Ask the class to say why the second approach is more effective in this case. Answers might include: *she got the result she wanted.* Use the audio script to check your answers.

Ⓓ Ask pairs to choose one of the scenarios in the exercise. They should decide on either the push or pull approach, confidentially, and write a short dialogue around this scenario, to be performed in front of the class. As the role plays are performed, ask the other students to note down specific phrases used and decide which approach each pair has used.

▶ FOR DEVELOPMENT AND CONSOLIDATION OF THE LANGUAGE ABOVE, SEE PAGE 17 OF THE WORKBOOK.

▶ REFER STUDENTS TO PAGE 148 OF THE COURSEBOOK FOR A SUMMARY OF THE POINTS COVERED IN THIS COMMUNICATION SECTION.

Business across Cultures

Motivation at work

Most of this section is based on McClelland's Motivational Needs theory. For background reading on David McClelland and his theory visit the following website:
http://en.wikipedia.org/wiki/David_McClelland

Ask students to open their books and cover up all of page 20 except for the introduction. Read the introduction together and ask students if they can guess (discourage them from looking further down the page) what the three motivational needs are.

Ⓐ Ask small groups to brainstorm factors that motivate them to work hard either professionally or as students. Get them to list their ideas on a flipchart to present to the rest of the class. Keep the presentations brief by limiting each one to 5 minutes.

Ⓑ Check understanding of *affiliation*. Instruct students to discuss the question in pairs. Ask two or three students to summarise their discussion to the rest of the class.

Ⓒ Students should brainstorm the characteristics and behaviour in small groups then share their ideas with the rest of the class. Afterwards, allow them to compare their answers with those on page 129.

KEY

*A person's need for **power** can be one of two types – personal and institutional. Those who need personal power want to direct others, and this need often is perceived as undesirable. Persons who need institutional power want to organise the efforts of others to further the goals of the organisation. Managers with a high need for institutional power tend to be more effective than those with a high need for personal power.*

*People with a high need for **achievement** seek to excel and tend to avoid both low-risk and high-risk situations. Achievers avoid low-risk situations because the easily attained success is not a genuine achievement. Achievers need regular feedback in order to monitor the progress of their achievements. They prefer either to work alone or with other high achievers.*

D This question can be discussed in pairs. Ask two or three students to report back to the class.

Power

E AUDIO **3.3** Read the introduction and go through the exercise and the statements with the class to check understanding. Play the audio once and get students to compare their answers in pairs. Do a class answer check.

KEY

1 T

2 F They didn't get involved.

3 F They didn't see the managers very often.

4 T

5 T

6 T

7 T

8 T

9 F She works with them. They are her clients.

10 T

11 F They treat freelancers badly.

AUDIO SCRIPT

1

I used to work for a large cement company, owned by the state. There was a strong hierarchy. The top men were all party members and they had the power. They would have their meetings and we would see their chauffeurs waiting outside to drive them to some other important meeting. We didn't see them very often. They didn't get involved in the dirty business of making cement. I was a shift supervisor and it was my job to make sure we produced on time and met our customer orders. It wasn't easy, as the machinery was always breaking down.

Three years ago we were bought by a French company and since then, things have changed a lot. Yes, there are the big bosses with the chauffeurs back in Paris, but I've met the managers here and they are very good. They give us very clear targets and support us in achieving them. I've been promoted to Operations Manager and I think they will leave the site for me to manage soon. The company has invested a lot in new equipment and also training.

2

For many years I worked as a designer in a small fashion house. I wasn't paid very well but they were a nice group of people. Then they went bankrupt, and I was made redundant so I decided to go freelance. I now work with some of the top fashion houses – they are my clients. It's not easy as there are some real 'prima donnas' in the fashion industry – people who take themselves too seriously. Personally I'm not at all status conscious but I have to recognise that some of the people I work with are. Some of them are very ambitious and try to make their mark by bossing around poor freelancers like me. It's not just the men either. Often the women are worse. The power seems to go their heads!

F This could be done as a whole group exercise.

G Instruct students to discuss this in pairs and encourage them to give reasons for their preferences. Ask three or four individuals to report what they and their partners said. Use the audio script to check your answers.

Personal and professional achievement

H Read the introduction and instructions together. Check understanding of *community spirit*. Give students time to read about the four entrepreneurs individually and check understanding if necessary. Ask them to work with a partner and discuss which factors drive each entrepreneur. Get students to compare their responses with the rest of the class.

KEY

1 Community spirit

2 Quality

3 Money

4 Size

I Divide the class into small groups to discuss this question. Afterwards, ask one person from each group to summarise their discussion.

Affiliation

J AUDIO **3.4** Read the introduction and the instructions together. Play the audio once and ask students to compare their answers with a partner. Do a class answer check.

KEY

colleagues   suppliers   investors

AUDIO SCRIPT

For me, work is all about relationships. That's why I go to work. I couldn't stand working from home. Who would I talk to? The dog I suppose. When I arrive at work, I have coffee with my assistant, Debs. We talk about the weekend, our kids, you know, that sort of thing. A couple of times a week the whole team has an informal meeting. It could be just standing around the coffee machine and catching up on things. In purchasing, it's our job to build partnerships with our vendors. Of course the decision to choose one company or another is based on price, delivery, etc. But in the end the critical question is, Can we work together? So I see our partners a lot. I'll call in or invite them over and in some cases we'll see each other socially in the evenings.

K Ask students to do the exercise in pairs as indicated in the Coursebook. If there's time, you could ask students to try to come up with other questions relating to relationships at work.

▶ FOR A QUIZ TO ASSESS YOUR MOTIVATIONAL NEEDS SEE PAGE 18 OF THE WORKBOOK.

▶ REFER STUDENTS TO PAGE 151 OF THE COURSEBOOK FOR A SUMMARY OF THE POINTS COVERED IN THIS BUSINESS ACROSS CULTURES SECTION.

▶ FOR FURTHER EXPLORATION OF MOTIVATION AT WORK AND CULTURE CLASH, SEE PHOTOCOPIABLE MATERIALS 1.3, PAGE 111.

Checklist

Review the end of unit checklist items in the Coursebook with your students, as well as the unit word field. Add any interesting pronunciation items to the pronunciation file started in Unit 1.

Extension activity: Referring the class to the listening section on independent working and the grammar section on conditionals, ask students to write a short article about what they would do if they had the opportunity to be self-employed in any field of their choosing. Encourage them to think about why (using reasons based on past experience for example), how, where, etc., and imagine what positive effects this would have on their life, or what possible risks might lie ahead. Encourage them to use the full range of conditionals. This could be done as a homework exercise and read out to the class after private review and correction.

Extension activity: Weak vowel sounds
Refer students back to the final activity on page 16 of the Teachers' Resource Book (Unit 1) which focused on stressed syllables. Explain that another problem with pronunciation is often the overstressing of the weak syllables in a word.

Write the following vocabulary items on the board with dots above where indicated.

o   o   o   o   o o   o   o   o
Americans freelancer contractor communication influence serious

Elicit the correct pronunciation pattern for these words from the class and ask them to say which sound they hear under the dots. Tell the class that this is the most common weak vowel sound, ə, which is a sound called 'Schwa'. Explain that over pronunciation of this weak vowel form can severely distort pronunciation and reduce the effect of strong syllables in speech.

Explain that the other two most important weak vowel sounds are /iː/ as in 'happy' and /uː/ as in influence. Divide the class into three groups. Ask each group to use the vocabulary word field compiled whilst studying this unit, or previous units, to find a few other examples of words with either the schwa or /iː/ or /uː/ weak vowel sounds and mark them in above each word. Do a class review and pronunciation practice of the vocabulary items found.

4 Are you being served?

Listening and speaking	The subject of standards of service and customer satisfaction levels in the public and private sector is presented in an interview with Laura Wright.
Grammar	**relative clauses** Students tackle the differences between defining and non-defining relative clauses in this section.
Reading and vocabulary	In this section, verb / noun collocations such as, *face challenges*, are presented in a report about public and private sector customer services.
Communication	**getting your message across** In this section students practise *packaging* their message for clearer communication.
Business cross Cultures	**organisational cultures** Students examine different organisational cultures and their advantages and disadvantages.

Start-up

A Ask the class to turn to page 22 of their Coursebooks. Check students' understanding of the difference between public and private. Ask students to tell you which of the businesses in A are public and which are private, or both. If you have a multinational class, form sub-groups by nationality.

B Direct students' attention to the statement about competition in public and private sector companies at the top of the page, elicit the meaning of *monopoly* and find out students' opinions on that statement. Answers might include words such as: *enormous, inefficient, corrupt.*

Listening and speaking

A Ask sub-groups (by nationality if applicable) to discuss which type of organisation they generally get the best service from, public or private, and report their decisions back to the class. Allow some time for comparison of different groups' experiences. Answers might include: *more efficient, more customer focused, more competitive, less bureaucratic, too much time and money spent competing with rivals.* Get students to begin a word field around the subject of *customer service.*

B Ask students to consider the benefits and drawbacks of privatising services which are currently public.

C [AUDIO **4.1**] Tell the class they are going to listen to a radio interview with Laura Wright about public and private services. They should decide whether the statements are true or false. Do a class answer check.

KEY

1 F *It is only managing the supply chain for the NHS.*
2 F *They spend less time in the stock room and more time on patient care.*
3 T
4 F *There are no rival companies offering alternative services to the same destination.*
5 T
6 F *They have dramatically improved. It used to be very expensive and customers had to wait years to be connected.*

AUDIO SCRIPT

Interviewer: With consumers more likely to complain when faced with poor service, the pressure is on both the public and private sectors to perform well and meet rising and changing customer demands. However, the public sector in particular is in the spotlight for not delivering what we want as consumers. Its critics are calling for it to adopt private sector methods. With me in the studio today is Laura Wright, a management consultant who regularly works with both the public and private sector. Laura, can state-run organisations copy the methods of private sector companies?

Laura Wright: To a certain extent, yes. There is a great deal that public sector organisations can learn from private sector methods.

Interviewer: Could you give us some examples?

Laura Wright: Of course. Let's look at the National Health Service here in the UK. It's adopted private sector methods in supply chain management. For those listeners not familiar with this, supply chain management is the way that an organisation obtains and manages the supplies that it needs in order to run its operations. DHL, the German company which is usually associated with delivery services, is managing the supply chain for the NHS by applying its commercial experience and logistics know-how. So, they source the high quality goods, manage contracts with suppliers, and take care of inventory and distribution. Through this, the NHS has reduced costs and increased efficiency. Now, clinical staff can spend less time in the stock room and more time on patient care. So we know that adopting certain private sector methods can improve inefficient services, but problems occur when some state-run services are completely transformed into private sector services.

Interviewer: So you're saying that not all industries benefit from privatisation and free market competition?

Laura Wright: That's right. Services which provide social benefits tend not to thrive under private ownership. In these industries you often have a monopoly situation, which means that there's no room for competition or choice – there is one provider who can charge what they like. The most straightforward way of ensuring fair prices and safe standards is through state provision – the state provides the services itself.

Interviewer: Right. So are there any industries which have been privatised that perhaps would have been better left in the state's hands?

Laura Wright: Oh, yes. A classic example of this is the privatisation of the UK railways, which actually resulted in a series of private monopolies. For instance, if you are travelling from London to Manchester by train, you can't choose how you get there – there are no rival companies offering alternative services to the same destination. So the trains are running later and later, and fares are rising faster than ever. In an attempt to improve the situation for passengers, the government tried to introduce competition but the rail industry is – by its very nature – monopolised. Unfortunately, the government's intervention has fragmented management control, created a further decline in quality, and produced unreliable and unsafe systems. Then there's the water industry, which has been a total failure for similar reasons ...

Interviewer: I see. So, can you give an example of a successful privatisation?

Laura Wright: Yes, in fact, I can. The privatisation of telecoms, for instance, is seen as a successful transformation by consumers all over the world. Latin America is becoming an explosive market for telecoms, in particular, Brazil and Argentina. In 1998, the Brazilian government, which was trying to gain popularity before the elections, sold off Telebras, the state-run phone company, because it wanted to create serious competition in the telecommunications field. When Telebras was state-run, customers applying for a phone line had to pay thousands of dollars in start-up fees and wait for years for the service while the paperwork was being processed. Now getting a line takes less than a week. Not only has privatisation improved services but it has contributed towards greater economic stability and has had a favourable impact on the Latin America stock exchange.

Extension activity: This audio script is rich in business collocations. Write the verbs in the first box below up on the left hand side of the board randomly and the expressions in the second box below up on the right hand side of the board. Divide the class into two groups. Get each group to use the words on opposite sides of the board. Ask students to listen to the excerpt once more and note which nouns the verbs or expressions on their side of

the board appear with. Do a class answer check and get the class to note down the other group's collocations. Use the audio script to check your answers. Add relevant items to the unit word field.

meet adopt obtain run apply manage source take care of reduce increase fragment

supply chain logistics inventory and state-run free market social rival explosive

D Divide the class into small groups to discuss their opinions on the level of customer service from the types of organisations mentioned in the question, and whether they have ever had to complain about any of them. They should briefly report their discussions back to the class and add any useful vocabulary added to the *customer service* word field.

E The structure of each presentation should consist of one slide outlining the customer service problems and another slide outlining proposed improvement strategies. Get students to do the exercise as instructed in the Coursebook and present their plan to the class. Encourage post-presentation questions and additional service improvement suggestions from the audience. Add any useful vocabulary to the unit word field. The following plan can be written up on the board and used as a model:

Example plan
Telephone call centre based in Glasgow, Scotland:
Customer service complaints:
- Takes too long to answer enquiries
- Operators speak very quickly
- Customers get cut off when being transferred to another adviser / service
- Try to sell other services whenever a customer calls

Customer service improvement plan:
- Employ more staff
- Give staff communication training and ask them to slow down
- Make technical improvements to call system
- Change product marketing policy

Grammar
Relative clauses
Run through the presented grammar rules for relative clauses with the class.

A Ask students to complete the exercise in the Coursebook and do a class answer check.

KEY
1 that public sector organisations can learn from private sector methods. (defining)
2 that an organisation obtains and manages the supplies (defining) that it needs in order to run its operations (defining)
3 which provide social benefits (defining)
4 which was trying to gain popularity before the elections (non-defining)

30

B Get students to complete these sentences in pairs. Do an open round for the class answer check, collecting sample endings.

Possible answers

1 *are controlled / run / managed by the government*

2 *work in the private sector*

3 *that there is no competition / that they can charge whatever they like for a product or service, etc.*

4 *has been kept in the public sector / is usually in the public sector / hasn't been privatised, etc.*

5 *is a genuine market / is in the public sector in many countries, etc.*

Extension activity: Ask half the class to write a very short article containing a maximum of ten sentences about a private sector organisation in their country. They should use only defining clauses. Ask the other half to do the same for a public sector organisation, using only non-defining clauses. This part could be done as a homework exercise. Review and correct each article, privately. Students should then read out their article to the class who should state whether it contains defining or non-defining clauses. Students should then rewrite their articles, using the other form of relative clause, as a homework exercise if necessary.

▶ FOR FURTHER INFORMATION ON RELATIVE CLAUSES, REFER STUDENTS TO GRAMMAR OVERVIEW, PAGE 156 OF THE COURSEBOOK.

▶ FOR SELF-STUDY EXERCISES ON RELATIVE CLAUSES, SEE PAGE 21 OF THE WORKBOOK.

▶ GRAMMAR REVIEW AND DEVELOPMENT, PAGE 32 OF THE COURSEBOOK, CAN BE DONE AT THIS STAGE.

Reading and vocabulary

A Elicit personal examples of complaints students have made about poor service. If you have a multicultural class, encourage class discussion about the culture of complaint, which can vary greatly between cultures. Elicit how complaints are generally made in each culture represented in your class. Answers might include: *letter, phone call, email, solicitor's letter.* Then elicit what sort of response is commonly given. Answers might include: *letter of apology, refund, vouchers for future products, bill reduction.*

B Ask the class to complete the exercise individually and do a quick class comprehension check.

KEY

1a   2d   3e   4c   5b

C Tell students to do the exercise as instructed in the Coursebook and do a class check of answers. Add useful vocabulary to the unit word field.

KEY

1 *People are more likely to complain when faced with poor service.*

2 *There is a greater awareness of consumer rights and people are more confident about speaking up for themselves when they experience poor customer service.*

3 *In implementing customer service initiatives, such as self-service systems and self-learning tools that organise and present customer information.*

4 *Lack of budgets and failure to understand the importance of customer service.*

D Run through the points in the exercise with the class and ask pairs to discuss them. Allow time for class discussion. Add any useful vocabulary to the unit word field.

▶ VOCABULARY REVIEW AND DEVELOPMENT, PAGE 32 OF THE COURSEBOOK, CAN BE DONE AT THIS STAGE.

▶ FOR FURTHER READING AND VOCABULARY PRACTICE RELATING TO THE TOPIC OF SERVICE, DIRECT STUDENTS TO PAGE 19 OF THE WORKBOOK.

Communication

Getting your message across

Ask students to turn to page 25 of their Coursebooks. Read through the opening paragraph with the class. Elicit any examples of situations in which students experienced very confused communication. Direct the class to look at the photo. Elicit reasons why people can often have problems communicating on the telephone. Answers might include:

language difficulties, more / less direct style of communication, bad line, no body language.

A AUDIO **4.2** Ask the class to listen to the audio and discuss the answers in pairs, before doing a class comprehension check. Elicit the fact that Pablo packages his difficult message well by using little phrases which introduce the subject gently.

KEY

1 *A member of the team isn't right for the job. He also wants to discuss the project management tool they are using.*

B Ask a student to read out the Key language to the class. Check understanding and review the fact that these language items help to introduce and 'package' the message. Tell the class to turn to page 116 of the Coursebook to do the exercise as instructed and play the audio script a second time.

KEY

Use the audio script to check your answers.

AUDIO SCRIPT

A: *Pablo, how are you?*

B: *Fine, thank you Carrie. And you?*

A: *Great. So what can I do for you?*

B: *Well, Carrie, I wanted to talk to you about the project.*

A: *Fine. How's it going?*

B: *Well, that's why I'm calling. There are some problems. In fact, there are two big problems.*

A: *Really?*

B: *Yes I'm worried. The first concerns one of the team, Martine Casals, and the other is more technical. You will remember that we asked Martine to join the team as a financial process expert?*

A: *Yes, I do. We needed someone to set up good cost control systems.*

B: *That's right. Unfortunately, she has proved to be the wrong person. I think she has a few personal problems at the moment and she's been upsetting the rest of the team.*

A: *I see. But can she do her job?*

B: *That's difficult to say but she's certainly not delivering at the moment. I'd like to make a proposal. I'd like to take her off the project and move her back into her old job. I have spoken to her old boss and that seems possible.*

A: *Right. You're the one on the ground. If you think that's best, let's go with that. How are you going to replace her?*

B: *Well, just before we come to that. Can I tell you about the other issue because I think we could solve them together?*

A: *Shoot.*

B: *So, it concerns the project management tool we are using. As you know it's PRO-GOAL and I think we can upgrade it to include a financial control module …*

Extension activity: Refer students back to the final activity in Unit 2. Elicit that when packaging the message with these phrases, intonation and pausing form an important part of the phrase. Ask pairs to act out the script, paying particular attention to these points.

C Ask pairs to do the exercise as instructed in the Coursebook. Get a few pairs to role play their scenarios in front of the class and ask the audience to note down and give feedback on the target language used. To review and give students feedback on any of the skills in Module 1, refer to the Communication Style Feedback framework on page 121.

▶ FOR DEVELOPMENT AND CONSOLIDATION OF THE LANGUAGE ABOVE, SEE PAGE 22 OF THE WORKBOOK.

▶ REFER STUDENTS TO PAGE 148 OF THE COURSEBOOK FOR A SUMMARY OF THE POINTS COVERED IN THIS COMMUNICATION SECTION.

▶ COMMUNICATION REVIEW AND DEVELOPMENT EXERCISES, PAGE 33 OF THE COURSEBOOK, CAN BE DONE AT THIS STAGE.

Business across Cultures

Organisational cultures

There are many theories about organisational culture (or 'corporate culture'), and the main theorist is Charles Handy, an Irish author and philosopher (Exercise E in this section is based on his ideas). You can find a very comprehensive overview of this area on the following website:
http://en.wikipedia.org/wiki/corporate_culture

For a link to a radio programme in which Charles Handy talks about his theories, go to:
http://www.onepine.info/phand.htm

A Read the introduction in class. Instruct students to discuss the question in pairs. Set a strict time limit as this is only a warm-up exercise. Ask two or three students to briefly summarise what their partner told them.

B AUDIO 4.3 Read through the instructions in class. Draw students' attention to the table. You may need to play the audio twice to allow students enough time to write their notes. Ask students to compare their notes with a partner then check their answers in class.

KEY

FSC	BBN
Working on study of obesity in children	**Advise Central Marketing Department on food safety issues**
Bureaucratic and slow	*Less research and more report writing*
Wait a long time for approval and feedback on projects	*Give people a lot of independence*
Works alone on projects	*Lots of commercial pressures*
	Tight financial targets and budgets
	Work as part of a dynamic team

AUDIO SCRIPT

Regula Tschudin: So Marco, can you tell me what you like about your current job?

Marco Pestalozzi: I really like my job and I have some interesting projects. At the moment, I am working on a study of obesity in children. It's very important work.

Regula Tschudin: I'm sure. If you join us, you would be attached to our Central Marketing Department and be advising them on food safety issues. You would be doing less research than you do in your current job and writing more summaries of reports.

Marco Pestalozzi: I realise that. I think a change will be good for me. To be honest, the FSC is very bureaucratic and slow.

Regula Tschudin: Yes, I can imagine. Certainly we like to think we are not so bureaucratic. We give our people a lot of independence and expect a lot from them in return. I think you would find this a very different place to work. There are a lot of commercial pressures and we have very tight financial targets and budgets.

Marco Pestalozzi: I like the idea that it will be very different and. I am used to working under quite strict budget constraints. What is really frustrating is that we wait for so long for approval for our projects and then when we finish them we wait even longer for any feedback or action – in fact, often we don't get any at all.

Regula Tschudin: Yes, that must be frustrating. Do you usually work in a team?

Marco Pestalozzi: Not really. Of course, I am part of a department and I report to the manager but usually I work alone on projects.

Regula Tschudin: It'll be very different here as you'd be joining a dynamic marketing team and we will be looking for your contribution to that team.

C Get students to interview each other about their work or study experiences. Ensure that they ask each other <u>full</u> questions. Afterwards, ask each pair to summarise the main differences and similarities between their experiences.

KEY

1 *person culture*

2 *role culture*

3 *power culture*

4 *task culture*

D Get students to do this exercise in pairs. Do a class answer check.

E Look at the diagrams together then ask a different student to read about each culture in front of the rest of the class. Check understanding as you go along. Some students may not understand the concept of *matrix basis*. (This combines functional and divisional structures. For example, an employee reports to a general manager within his division as well as a functional manager at a central location who oversees that function across all divisions.) Get other students to provide definitions if possible. Get students to do the exercise in pairs then check answers in class.

F Ask students to do the exercise in pairs then compare their answers with the rest of the class.

KEY

1 Task culture   2 Role culture   3 Person culture
4 Power culture

G Assign two cultures to each group and get them to focus on the advantages and disadvantages of those cultures. Get the groups to write the advantages and disadvantages on a flipchart and then present their ideas to the class. Invite comments and questions from the other students.

Here are some possible responses:

POWER CULTURE

<u>Advantages</u>	<u>Disadvantages</u>
Organisation	
Dynamic	*Staff dissatisfaction*
Can react quickly to external demands	*If the judgement of the central power is poor, the organisation will suffer*
Employee	
–	*No decision-making power*

ROLE CULTURE

<u>Advantages</u>	<u>Disadvantages</u>
Organisation	
Predictable	*Inflexibility*
Stable	*Difficulty adjusting to change*
Employee	
Security/Predictability	*No opportunity for innovation*

TASK CULTURE

<u>Advantages</u>	<u>Disadvantages</u>
Organisation	
Flexible	*Projects involve high risk*
	Can only control projects through reviews, target setting, budgets and resource allocations
	Interdependence is required for the organisation to function properly
Employee	
Have control over own work	*Low morale if individual priorities are not met e.g. sufficient budget*
Decision-making power	*or resources*

PERSON CULTURE

<u>Advantages</u>	<u>Disadvantages</u>
Organisation	
–	*The organisation has no objectives except to support the 'individuals' within it*
	Impossible to control and coordinate all of the 'individuals'
Employee	
The organisation is simply a base on which s/he can build his/her own career	
Preserves own identity	

Extension activity: This activity would work well with a creative class. Tell your students that Charles Handy, an Irish author and philosopher came up with the organisational culture theory (power culture, task culture, etc.) above. Explain that he used four Greek gods to symbolise these cultures:

Zeus Culture (Power culture) →
the powerful head of the gods.

Apollo Culture (Role culture) →
the God of harmony, reason and order.

Athena Culture (Task culture) →
the warrior goddess represents the ideal manager whose main motivation is to get the job done properly.

Dionysus Culture (Person culture) →
the self-oriented deity.

Ask students to form small groups and brainstorm other metaphors for the four cultures. Encourage them to use elements of their own cultures as metaphors and explain that they can be as outlandish as they like provided they can justify their ideas. Get each group to present their metaphors to the rest of the class, giving reasons for their choices.

After the exercise, reveal the following metaphors that have been used:

Power culture – A spider's web with a ruling spider at the centre.

Task culture – A net. Structured yet flexible and easy to 'shape' depending on the task.

Role culture – A temple. Its columns represent the different departments which are controlled by strict procedures. Decisions are made and conflicts are resolved at the 'pediment'.

Person culture – Galaxies containing lots of individual stars.

▶ FOR A READING ACTIVITY ON RECENT GRADUATES 'FITTING IN' IN DIFFERENT ORGANISATIONAL CULTURES SEE PAGE 23 OF THE WORKBOOK.

▶ REFER STUDENTS TO PAGE 151 OF THE COURSEBOOK FOR A SUMMARY OF THE POINTS COVERED IN THIS BUSINESS ACROSS CULTURES SECTION.

Checklist

Review the end of unit checklist items in the Coursebook with your students, as well as the unit word field. Add any interesting pronunciation items to the pronunciation file started in Unit 1. To review relative clauses, give each student a slip of paper. Divide the class in two. Ask half the class to write a sentence containing a defining clause, and the other half to write one containing a non-defining clause, relating to their organisation, on their slip of paper. Tell them to make no give-away references to their organisation, such as names, products, etc. Circulate, reviewing and correcting each student's sentence. Take in the slips of paper. Read them out to the class, and ask students to guess who wrote it, awarding points to the student who gets the most correct answers.

Extension activity: Explain that spoken English is most effectively delivered and received in small, manageable blocks rather than long, unpunctuated sentences. These blocks are punctuated by pauses. Instruct the class to turn to audio script 4.1 on page 115 of the Coursebook. Tell the class to listen to the introduction and first question and answer in audio script 4.1 again, and mark their scripts where they hear natural pauses. Ask one pair to read out this section of the interview script, pausing where appropriate. Then, elicit that not all

33

pauses are of the same length. Whilst the more dramatic pauses usually occur where punctuation occurs in the script, there are other slightly less dramatic pauses which occur naturally, to make understanding easier.

Assign the remaining four questions and answers to different pairs. Ask pairs to mark a // where they imagine there is a more significant pause, and a / where there is a slightly shorter pause. Then play the audio script and get them to check their answers. Finally get a different pair to read out each question and answer, pausing appropriately. If possible, audio recording these mini interviews will aid review.

An element of humour can be introduced by recording pairs doing their mini interviews without pauses or with pauses in all the wrong places, before they record their correct version, to show the negative effect of poorly punctuated delivery.

Business Scenario 1

MEDIACO

This Business Scenario incorporates the themes of leadership, teamwork, and job satisfaction which appear in Units 1 and 2. During the speaking task, students are required to use conditional sentences, which are presented in Unit 3, to describe how they would improve morale in Mediaco. The language task introduces phrases that are used to express opinions about various options. The students use them to discuss solutions to the problem of morale and motivation. The role play takes the form of a meeting between an external consultant and the CEO and HR Director of Mediaco. This provides students with the opportunity to use active listening techniques, which feature in the Communication section of Unit 2, in the context of a meeting. The writing task involves writing an email to employees explaining which procedures were selected during the meeting.

Introductory activity

Before students open their Coursebooks, ask them: *What are the causes of low morale in a team?*

Write their suggestions on the board.

Possible responses:

> *Poor management*
> *Poor rapport with other team members*
> *Employees not given enough responsibility*
> *Unclear goals*

Background

Ask students to open their Coursebooks on page 28 and read the background.

Speaking

To make students come up with their own ideas, ask them to cover the information about the meeting at the bottom of the page.

Write the following on the board:

> *If I were CEO ...*

Instruct students to discuss the question in pairs and use conditional sentences to describe what they *would do*. Instruct them to discuss this question in pairs. Allow five minutes then ask students to share their ideas with the rest of the class. Ensure that they use the conditional form correctly. Write their suggestions on the board and invite comments from other students.

Possible responses:

> *I'd ...*
> *... improve communication systems.*
> *... organise a teambuilding event.*
> *... arrange management training.*
> *... introduce incentive and benefit schemes.*

Once you have discussed the students' suggestions, ask them to read the information about the meeting at the bottom of the page.

Language

Look at the expressions together in class. You may wish to draw students' attention to the sentence stress in these expressions. For example:

> This would **really** help us to ...
>
> This is **just** what we need to ...
>
> What's the **point** of ...ing?

You could also elicit other ways of discussing the different options. For example:

There's no doubt that ... (to make statements stronger)

Before embarking on the exercise, elicit two or three example statements in class. Ask students to discuss the options in pairs for approximately five minutes. Circulate during the activity and correct their use of the expressions and sentence stress. Ask two or three students to provide examples after the exercise, then make corrections and provide feedback.

Role play

Prior to this activity, briefly review active listening techniques. Remind students that good listeners often gain trust more easily and are usually better negotiators. Can they remember some of the techniques? Write a few of their examples on the board.

Possible responses:

> *Open questions – What ...?*
> *Clarifying questions – So, you mean that ...?*
> *Confirming comments – I see.*
> *Showing interest – That sounds ...*
> *Summarising – Let me just make sure I've got the picture.*

Divide the class into groups of three and assign a role to each person. If you have an 'extra' student in the class, you could form a group of four and ask an imaginative student to invent his / her role (for example, a trade union representative). Ensure that you assign the Student A role to a confident student. Ask the 'candidates' to study their roles carefully and consider how best to present their arguments. Student As should consider ways of welcoming the candidates and ending the discussion. Allow plenty of time for preparation (up to 10 minutes). Warn students that they will need to take notes about any decisions made during their meetings as they will need this information to do the writing exercise below.

The discussions should have a strict time limit (20 minutes would be appropriate). Run the discussions simultaneously and, if possible, record each one on audio to analyse during feedback. Students often find it useful to observe their own strengths and weaknesses. However, do not spend too much time listening to the recordings as students are likely to lose interest. Try to use them selectively to highlight positive interaction and elicit areas that could be improved. It is important to ask students for their opinions about the meeting: *Did you achieve the aim of the meeting? Is everyone satisfied with the results? Did everyone have a chance to speak? Did you understand each other?*

Writing

Ask students what information they could include in Brian Owen's email.

For example:

Background information (anonymous questionnaire and findings)

Choice of procedures and reasons

Future action (promise to keep employees updated, for example)

Set the writing exercise for homework and correct / check them outside class. You could use two or three in class to highlight weaknesses and strengths common to the group.

Review and development 1–4

Vocabulary: Leadership characteristics

A Ask students to do this exercise in pairs. To make it fun, ask students to see which pair can complete the crossword correctly first. Ask them to put their hands in the air when they have finished, and check their answers. Compare answers and deal with any queries in class when everyone has completed the crossword.

KEY

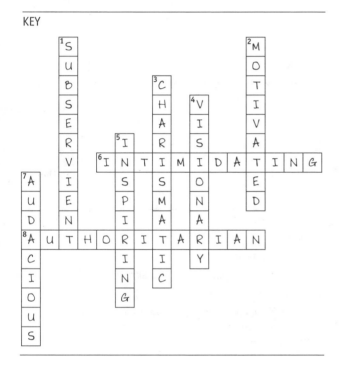

Grammar: Modals

A Write the following headings on the board and elicit which modal verbs are used to express these functions:

| Ability | Possibility | Deduction | Obligation |
| Past habits | Advice | | |

To review the present form of modals, write the following two sentences on the board and ask students which is correct:

You must to speak to Marian.

You must speak to Marian.

(Elicit the rule that modal verbs are always followed by the infinitive <u>without</u> 'to'.)

To review the past form of modals, write the following on the board:

Why wasn't John here last week?

I don't know. <u>He (go) on a business trip.</u>

Ask students to change the underlined part to express a deduction:

He <u>must/could/might/may have gone</u> on a business trip.

Get students to do both exercises A and B in pairs then compare their answers in class.

KEY
A 1 *would*   2 *could*   3 *must*   4 *shouldn't*   5 *must*
B 1 *past habits*   2 *prediction*   3 *deduction*   4 *advice*
   5 *obligation*

Vocabulary: Idioms

A This is best done individually or for homework.

KEY

A

1 *The programme did not have enough viewers, so the TV company <u>pulled</u> the plug on it.*

2 *I wanted to finish the proposal by this evening, but I've been rushed off my <u>feet</u> all day.*

3 *OK, let's stop talking about secondary issues and <u>cut</u> to the chase.*

4 *We've ignored the problems for a long time, but now we need to <u>face</u> the music.*

5 *The department is overstaffed: half the people there are not pulling their <u>weight</u>.*

6 *She was very quick to <u>take</u> the new situation on board.*

7 *I've been meaning to call you, but I've <u>had</u> a lot on my plate recently.*

8 *I need to touch <u>base</u> with the US office and let them know how things are going.*

Grammar: Conditionals

Before embarking on the exercises, elicit the rules for each type of conditional. Write up sentences to support them.

A/**B** Ask students to do these exercises in pairs then compare answers in class.

KEY
A 1b   2c   3a   4f   5d   6e
B 1 *third*   2 *zero*   3 *first*   4 *third*   5 *second*   6 *zero*

C Instruct students to do this exercise individually. While they are doing this, circulate and look out for any problems; make sure students punctuate their sentences correctly. They should then compare their sentences with a partner. Afterwards, ask five students to tell the rest of the class one of their sentences.

D This exercise should be set up in the same way as exercise C.

Extension activity:
If you wish to focus on the use of conditional sentences in bargaining, use the following activity.

Stage 1:
Write the following on the board:

Bargaining

If you pay me tomorrow, I'll give you a discount.

If you bought 200 items, I'd give you an extra 50 for free.

Then ask students:

Which is more tentative? In which sentence does the

speaker think the other person is very unlikely to agree?
(The second)

Write the following prompts on the board and elicit more bargaining sentences:

If you (do) your homework ...
If you (lend) me your car ...

Stage 2:
The negotiations
Write the following on the board:

A	►	B
You need <u>data</u> from B within 1 week		*Collating the data will take at least 2 weeks*
You have a budget of $3,000 if B incurs any expenses in meeting your deadline		*You want A to help you with a new contract*

Manufacturer	►	Mining industry
You want the mining industry to stop polluting the water you use		*You can offer up to $2 million in compensation* *You can reduce your emissions by 30%*

ABC Company	►	Works Council
You want to avoid a strike in the case of redundancies		*You want ABC to modernise its plant to secure existing jobs*

Check that students understand the contexts of the negotiations. You could elicit further details about each scenario. For example:

You: What do you think the manufacturer will do if the mining industry doesn't stop polluting the water?
Students: Go to the press. / Lobby the government. / etc.

Next tell students that they are going to role play the negotiations in pairs. Allow about 10 minutes for this and circulate to check use of bargaining language.

Stage 3:
Now ask students to discuss their negotiations using conditional sentences. For example: If you hadn't agreed to modernise the plant, more jobs would have been lost.

Give them five minutes to come up with as many sentences as possible then ask for a few examples during feedback.

Grammar: Relative clauses

A This is best done individually or for homework.

KEY
1 The drug <u>that</u> was invented last year will save thousands of lives.
2 The City is the leading financial centre in London, <u>where</u> you'll find hundreds of international banks.
3 Paul Bishop was a company executive <u>who</u> was shot in mysterious circumstances last year.
4 The privatisation of the post office, <u>which</u> has not been discussed much in the media, could be next.
5 The candidate <u>whose</u> CV was outstanding was offered the job.

Vocabulary: Verb–noun combinations

A/**B** These exercises are best done individually or for homework.

KEY
A 1c   2e   3d   4b   5a

B
1 exceeding quotas
2 implement safety measures
3 delivered fresh goods
4 resources were deployed
5 has faced / has been facing criticism

Communication

Ask students to study the communication skills pages in Units 9–12 for homework.

A Ask students to do this exercise in pairs then compare their responses in class.

Model answers
1 I'm afraid I'm not sure about this.
2 I really feel we need to review the system.
3 So, have you thought about the next step?
4 I thought the performance was fantastic.
5 Hi, you must be Geoff. How's life treating you?

B Once again, ask students to do this exercise in pairs then compare their responses in class.

Model answers
1 What sort of work do you do?
2 Really! (show interest)
3 So, a big part of your job is food safety?
4 I see.
5 OK, so if I understand you, there are two main issues: firstly demanding legislation and secondly, team management.

C Ask one student to read the text to the rest of the class. Ask students whether it uses a push or pull approach and why.

KEY
Push
Afterwards, elicit the main features of each approach:

<u>Push</u>	<u>Pull</u>
Be well prepared	Negotiate the objective
Make sure the objective is clear etc.	Use questions to lead the process etc.

(Further information can be found in the Communication section on page 148.)

D Ask students to do the exercise as indicated in pairs. Get them to compare their answers in class.

E Preparation for this exercise could be set for homework. Ask half the class to do it using the push approach and the other half to do it using the pull approach.

If you have a very large class, ask students to give their individual presentations in groups of four. Circulate during the exercise and make a note of the language used. During feedback, ask two confident students (one with a push approach and the other with a pull approach) to give their presentations again in front of the whole class. Finally, provide feedback and corrections.

Markets

MODULE OVERVIEW

AIMS AND OBJECTIVES

Module 2 examines the area of markets, exploring the issues relating to entering foreign markets, finding a unique selling proposition for your company, choosing the right brand strategy and how companies advertise to both niche and mass markets. The grammar and functions reflect elements of these themes; the passive structures to describe industrial processes, a sophisticated range of modifying phrases are practised to make more accurate comparisons and a range of phrases are used to talk about future probabilities. The communication sections aim to develop a more advanced presentation style, focusing students on engaging their audience more effectively by asking them questions or referring to the audience's needs or situation, and a more professional approach to interviewing and giving feedback, through the use of questions. The Business across Cultures sections begin with India's culture and values with a particular focus on attitudes towards time. Next, students explore 'dress' in relation to attitudes towards dress and what dress says about a person in different cultures. Finally, this module looks at branding nations, the means of measuring, building and branding the reputation of countries, and global marketing.

At the end of this module, students should be able to:
- discuss the advantages and disadvantages of different ways of entering markets
- understand design, production and delivery processes
- compare brands and brand strategies of local and global brands
- understand the advantages and disadvantages of product placement
- use a range of determiners and quantifiers accurately
- use the passive structures to describe industrial processes
- use a sophisticated range of modifying phrases to make more accurate comparisons
- use a range of phrases to talk about future probabilities
- relate more effectively to their presentation audience
- conduct more comfortable and productive interviews
- give feedback in a more people-friendly and empowering way
- identify different attitudes towards time and dress and how they can influence doing business with another culture
- understand what is involved in branding nations
- understand how culture affects marketing

THEMATIC OVERVIEW

The themes in this module are interlinked through their association with the word *markets*. Looking overseas to vast emerging markets for cheaper production partnerships and, more importantly, enormous new sales territory opportunities, is a risky venture. There are many ways of trying to get into new markets and many have had their corporate fingers burnt in the process. Success is not guaranteed, although the potential rewards are tempting. In an increasingly superficial and yet sophisticated age in which the consumer is constantly bombarded by attractive purchasing propositions from all sides, the marketing industry is having to find ever more subtle and persuasive ways to make sure the consumer identifies a need for their product. Once you've got the product or service and found the right USP to give your product a branding edge, how do you go about advertising it? Which forms of media do you use? Product placement can send the consumer subliminal messages that your product is a 'must have'.

MAIN AUDIO CONTENTS

UNIT 5: talk by an export manager about three different ways of getting into new markets; several presentation introduction extracts; interview about doing business in India.

UNIT 6: several presentation introduction extracts; dialogue in which advice is given on what type of dress to wear in the UK.

UNIT 7: four extracts of consumers comparing local and global brands; job interview for a marketing position; a short extract from an interview in which an advisor defines nation branding; interview about nation branding in the developing world.

UNIT 8: two interviews with an advertising executive about reaching the Hispanic market; extract from a performance review interview; three extracts in which speakers describe how different markets have resisted globalisation.

PHOTOCOPIABLE RESOURCES (PAGES 113–117)

2.1 should be used just before task H in the Business across Cultures section of Unit 5.
2.2 can be used any time after Unit 7 and 14.
2.3 can be used any time after Unit 8.

BUSINESS AND CULTURAL NOTES

These sections aim to highlight values and assumptions that often cause misunderstandings in the international business environment. For instance, some cultures are very time-dominated whereas others, such as India, are less led by the clock. As one would expect, this leads to confusion and anxiety in relation to scheduling, staging and delivering international projects. In a multicultural class, students brief the rest of the class on attitudes towards time in their own culture. The objective of this is to raise awareness that one's own assumptions are not always shared by people from other cultures. Students also explore the issue of disputes concerning 'appropriate' dress through discussion and role plays.

5 Entering new markets

Vocabulary and listening

The vocabulary in this section deals with different ways of entering markets, such as *licensing* and *franchising*. This vocabulary features in a listening exercise in which an export manager talks about the advantages and disadvantages of different methods.

Reading and speaking

This section deals with the successes and failures of joint overseas ventures.

Grammar

determiners and quantifiers

Determiners and quantifiers and the nouns they precede, are tackled in this section.

Communication

presentations: Engaging your audience 1

This section gets students to identify and practise different ways of involving the audience in a presentation.

Business cross Cultures

India

In this section, students examine the cross-cultural challenges of doing business in India, such as different attitudes towards time and hierarchy.

Introductory activity

With Coursebooks closed, ask the class to estimate the total value of international trade per minute. Instruct the class to open their Coursebooks at page 34 and read the opening statement to find out how close they were to the answer. Ask them to look at the photo and elicit that it shows a foreign brand which has entered an international market.

Start-up

A Ask pairs to do the exercise as instructed in the Coursebook, before a class review of their ideas.

Vocabulary and listening

A Check students' understanding of the meaning of *market entry* before asking students to do this exercise individually. Do a class answer check of the vocabulary and check comprehension and pronunciation of vocabulary such as *merge* and *intermediaries*. Refer the class back to one or two of the examples they gave in the start-up activity and elicit ways in which the companies entered the market.

KEY

1f   2c   3d   4e   5a   6b

B Ask pairs to do the exercise as instructed in the Coursebook, before a class review of their ideas. Universal answers might include: McDonald's, KFC – franchising.

Start up a unit word field around the word *markets*, with the six vocabulary items from A around it, and useful vocabulary relating to these items, attached to the relevant word.

C [AUDIO **5.1**] Do a quick review of the six methods of market entry in A. Tell the class that they are going to listen to an export manager talking about three different ways of getting into new markets and to match each extract to one of the methods in A.

KEY

1 Direct investment   2 Direct export   3 Licensing

D Ask the class to listen again for the advantages and disadvantages of each of the three methods and complete the table. Do a quick class answer check.

KEY

	Method	Advantage	Disadvantage
1	*Direct investment*	*All the profit is yours to keep, apart from tax paid in the country*	*Big gamble*
2	*Direct export*	*Get to know the market better*	*Expensive*
3	*Licensing*	*Don't have to make a big massive investment*	*Local partners might steal your idea*

If appropriate for your class, expand the discussion of this topic. For example: ask students to explain specific reasons why direct investment could be a big gamble. Answers might include: *lack of understanding of local skills levels, cultural values which affect the way of working, hidden infrastructure deficiencies, unstable or quickly changing economies.*

You could also ask students whether they agree or disagree with the stated disadvantage of expense for the direct export method. Answers might include: *risk is the biggest expense, setting up a foreign production facility is probably more expensive and riskier / most countries set up foreign production facilities where labour and other costs are cheaper so exporting from a richer country to a poorer one might not be a viable business proposition.*

Allow time for discussion and write up all useful language.

AUDIO SCRIPT

1 This approach involves opening your own facilities or subsidiaries in a new market. The good thing about it is that all the profits you make are yours to keep, well apart from tax paid in the country! Of course, it has its downsides. It's an enormous gamble – you might lose vast amounts of money if you misjudge things. But, who knows, one day, you might open a plant in China!

2 This method is better than having an export agent in the country as the key advantage is that it allows you to get to know the market better. A disadvantage is that it can be expensive. If you want to enter a market this way, you'll need your own export manager and you have to decide whether to send someone out there or recruit someone locally. The good thing with a local person is that they know the local market and the business culture.

3 And this is another way of getting into a new market: the advantage is you don't have to make a massive investment. This is an arrangement that we have used in some markets where earlier sales were promising. You've got to find good local partners and make sure you get a good lawyer for the contract. The only bad thing about this is that the local guys might steal your idea and then make the product by themselves without telling you!

E Ask pairs to do the exercise as instructed in the Coursebook and add useful phrases to the unit word field.

Example:
It has its downsides.

KEY

Use the audio script to check your answers.

F Elicit other expressions for advantages and disadvantages. Answers might include: *upsides, downsides, benefits, inconveniences, positives, negatives, attractions.*

▶ VOCABULARY REVIEW AND DEVELOPMENT, PAGE 60 OF THE COURSEBOOK, CAN BE DONE AT THIS STAGE.

Reading and speaking

A Refer the class back to the examples they gave of companies who have used joint ventures as a way of entering a new market. Ask pairs to discuss some of the advantages and disadvantages of joint ventures. Answers might include: *Advantages: local knowledge, corporate social responsibility good for business, local political support. Disadvantages: cultural misunderstandings in ways of working, language difficulties, variation in skills levels.* After a quick class review of ideas, add useful phrases to the unit word field.

B Read the title to the article. Elicit that *partnership* is a synonym of *joint venture* and that 'feel the Indian heat' suggests that these partnerships are not very successful. Instruct the class to read the article. Depending on your class, do a quick class check of difficult vocabulary items such as: *excavator, insisted, gain access to, mandatory, hold attractions for, inward investor, work out, push on, wholly owned.*

C Ask students to do the exercise as instructed in the Coursebook. Do a class answer check.

KEY

The order and answers are as follows:

d JCB was involved in a joint venture with an Indian company, Escorts. JCB ended its partnership as it likes to be in charge.

a India's regulation of foreign investment is becoming less severe as the Indian government has made it easier for foreign companies to have full control over their operations there.

c India still regulates foreign investment in industries such as telecommunications, agriculture, retailing and insurance.

e In TVS's collaboration with Suzuki, there were gains in both directions. TVS gained expertise and Suzuki could get into the market.

b TVS did not gain as much from its joint venture with Suzuki as it had hoped because Suzuki wanted to keep its technology for itself.

Extension activity: Write up the categories, *obligations and restrictions, success and failure, partnership synonyms,* on the board. Divide the class into three groups. Get each group to review the article for expressions relating to one of these categories. Ask students to come to the board and write up words and phrases as they find them. Add them to the unit word field attached to the appropriate category.

Suggested answers:
obligations and restrictions:
*to relax the rules   to insist   to make it easier to
to be required to   mandatory   government restrictions
the only way into the market*

success and failure:
*fantastic opportunities   to hold attractions for
to work out poorly/happily   potential problems
to gain   to get something from   frustrating
to make good progress*

partnership synonyms:
joint venture   collaboration   alliance   cooperation

D Give students time to review the article for appropriate arguments and do the exercise as instructed in the Coursebook. As some students may be using Best Practice Upper Intermediate Coursebook, and indeed business English for the first time, and as meetings language and procedure has not yet been tackled in the Coursebook, do this as a relatively informal pairwork exercise if necessary. If you have a meetings-experienced class, a more formal meeting with a larger number of participants is suggested. The Participating in Meetings Feedback framework on page 125 is really designed for use once the meetings communication sections have been tackled, but can be used at this stage to a certain extent.

▶ FOR FURTHER READING AND VOCABULARY PRACTICE RELATING TO THE TOPIC OF NEW MARKETS, DIRECT STUDENTS TO PAGE 24 OF THE WORKBOOK.

Grammar

Determiners and quantifiers

A Read the instruction with the class and ask the class to do the exercise as instructed in the Coursebook individually. Do a quick class answer check.

KEY

1 the   the

2 a   The

3 the   the   the   a   a

B Instruct the class to complete the text about joint ventures using the determiners in the box. Do a class answer check.

KEY

1 A

2 several

3 both

4 any

5 little

6 this

7 Another

8 other

9 enough

10 neither

C Instruct the class to look at the determiners in B again and complete the table individually. Do a class answer check.

KEY

Singular count	Plural count	Uncount
a	several	little
another	both	this*
neither	any	enough
	other	

*This can also be used with a singular count noun.

D Ask the class to discuss which quantifiers are grammatically correct in pairs. Do a class review of answers.

KEY

1 both of, neither of, all of

2 Many of, A few of

3 All of, Neither of

Extension activity: After a review of the target language, instruct pairs to write their own gapfill paragraph relating to their organisation or place of study, containing these determiners and quantifiers, with an answer key.
Alternatively get each student to do this individually as a homework exercise. Review and correct each gapfill with individuals. Get individuals to photocopy an uncompleted version of their gapfill and and exchange it with another student. He / she should complete the gapfill and check his / her answers with their partner.

▶ FOR FURTHER INFORMATION ON DETERMINERS AND QUANTIFIERS, REFER STUDENTS TO GRAMMAR OVERVIEW, PAGE 157 OF THE COURSEBOOK.

▶ FOR SELF-STUDY EXERCISES ON DETERMINERS AND QUANTIFIERS, SEE PAGE 26 OF THE WORKBOOK.

▶ GRAMMAR REVIEW AND DEVELOPMENT, PAGE 60 OF THE COURSEBOOK, CAN BE DONE AT THIS STAGE.

Communication

Presentations: Engaging your audience 1

With Coursebooks closed, explain that this section is the first of two sections designed to greatly improve the impact of your students' presentations. Ask small groups to brainstorm a short list of ways in which a presenter can make a real impact during a presentation. Do a class review of answers, which might include: *interesting topic, designed for audience, good introduction and conclusion, open body language, clear speech, well-structured and organised*. Write all ideas up on the board. Many of these aspects help to *engage an audience* so use this as a link to present the subject of this exercise.

A Elicit a few specific techniques for engaging the audience at the beginning of a presentation. Answers might include: *ask a question, present a fact which relates to them or to you*.

B Check students' understanding of vocabulary such as: *slides* and *beamer*. Ask the class to study the communication techniques in the table and elicit examples of where they have used or seen these techniques.

C AUDIO 5.2 Instruct the class to listen to two extracts from different presentations and decide which presentation engages the audience better. Play the audio and let students compare answers in pairs before asking them to explain their answers in detail to the rest of the class.

KEY

The second presentation engages the audience better.

D Tell students to listen to the second presentation again and to note down which techniques from the table the presenter uses to engage the audience. Do a class review of answers.

KEY

Use the audio script to check your answers.

AUDIO SCRIPT

1

Thank you for inviting me to this beautiful city and giving me the opportunity to talk to you. I will be updating you on recent developments in our new product pipeline and also looking forward to the next three years of development. Now, as you can see on this first slide, there are two main thrusts to our development plans. On the one hand ...

... So this next slide shows you the specific results we have had in the first area ...

... As you can see, there have been some quite dramatic breakthroughs. Now I'd like you to look at some more results, here we can see the ...

2

Thank you for inviting me to this beautiful city. I don't know if any of you have been to my part of the world – that's Scotland. No? Well I can understand why you would want to stay here! Now, I've come with a lot of results to show you from our latest research projects, but I've also put them on these handouts, so you can look at the detail later. What I'd really like to do is find out whether these projects fit in with your needs and that we are going in the right direction. So the first one, as you probably know, is on a new innovation in infant food formula. Now does this excite you? I mean, are you waiting for something like this?

Extension activity: Ask pairs to think of one or two more techniques which could be used for engaging the audience's attention and report them back to the class. Answers might include: *tell them an interesting fact / joke, show a picture slide and ask them about it.* Get the class to note down any new ideas.

E Review the techniques presented and brainstormed earlier and instruct students to prepare a five-minute presentation on one of the suggested topics. Depending on your class, students can choose their own topic. This could be prepared as a homework exercise.

F Ask students to deliver their short presentations. Get the rest of the class to note down the ways in which each presenter engages with their audience. Do a class feedback after each presentation. The Presentation Feedback framework on page 123 can be used.

▶ FOR DEVELOPMENT AND CONSOLIDATION OF THE LANGUAGE ABOVE, SEE PAGE 27 OF THE WORKBOOK.

▶ REFER STUDENTS TO PAGE 148 OF THE COURSEBOOK FOR A SUMMARY OF THE POINTS COVERED IN THIS COMMUNICATION SECTION.

Business across Cultures

India

To prepare for this section you can find some very insightful articles on cross-cultural issues and business in India on the following website created by a business consultant in Bangalore: www.arunkottolli.blogspot.com. There is also a very thorough overview of India and its culture on the following website: www.executiveplanet.com/index.php?title=india

Read the introduction together then ask students: *What do you think are the main challenges of doing business in India?*

A Ask students to do the quiz in pairs and compare their answers with the rest of the class as indicated in the Coursebook. Get students to check their answers on page 133.

KEY

1 c There is no official religion in India. India is a pluralist society and all religions have equal status, although Hinduism is the dominant religion.

2 Hindu	*80.5 per cent*
Muslim	*13.4 per cent*
Christian	*2.5 per cent*
Sikh	*1.9 per cent*
Buddhist, Jain, Parsi	*1.8 per cent*

3 b When Indians are in conversation or receiving instructions, they often shake their head from side to side, which to most Westerners looks like they are indicating disagreement; but they are simply indicating they are listening and understand what you say.

4 c There are over 400m cows in India, mostly in the countryside but some in the towns. Food for them is so scarce that they are sent to graze and eat what they can find. The fact they are left alone to wander along the street is because they are considered sacred by Hindus.

5 c The bindi that women wear is traditionally a sign of a married woman, but among young women in urban India it is now a fashion statement, and many different designs and colours can be found. It is also something only worn by Hindus, so to some extent all three options are true.

B Before reading the article, ask students what they know about the Indian and Chinese manufacturing industries. Which is the leader in this industry? China or India? Instruct students to read the article on their own. Afterwards, check understanding and deal with vocabulary questions by asking students to provide definitions of any problem words or expressions for each other. Next, ask them to answer the questions with a partner then compare answers in class.

KEY

2 Tax holidays, more control over infrastructure like water and power, and less regulation.

3 It's close to the market and there are many highly educated people there.

C Instruct students to do the exercise as indicated in the Coursebook. Provide flipchart paper for them to list their ideas on to present to the rest of the class. Encourage comments and questions from the 'audience'.

Some possible responses include:

Longer working hours

Different concepts of time (adherence to a strict schedule is not considered a priority)

The fact that Indians do not like to say 'no'

Indian respect for power and status

Indian lack of tolerance for public criticism

Different social conventions (for example, avoiding saying 'No' when declining an invitation)

Indian preference for deferring decisions

D Get students to compare their ideas in C with the subjects in the box. You may need to check the meaning of some of the words, such as *initiative* and *seniority*.

E **5.3** Play the audio and ask students to check their answers in pairs. Compare answers in class.

KEY

Time	Agreement	Seniority	Hierarchy
Family	Relationships		

AUDIO SCRIPT

A: *Arvind, can you tell us the secret of doing business in India?*

B: *Well, I think there are some cultural realities which are critical if you want to be successful in India. Coming from the West, you need to adapt to the Indian working day. The standard nine to five is not so different but generally we work six days with Sundays off. Some businesses give employees every other Saturday off, or make a shorter work day on Saturday.*

A: *Some people have a stereotype of India as a country which suffers from a lot of delays. Is that true?*

B: *I think it's true if you're dealing with the public sector. Government bureaucracy is well known and means things move at a slower pace. In the private sector, I think you'll find things happen at a fast pace, maybe even faster than the West. However, one thing which can lead to communication breakdown is that we don't like to say no. So it may be that an Indian agrees to do something or says 'I'll try' and in fact it's not realistic, so this can later lead to disappointment.*

A: *What about Indian companies? How do they work?*

B: *It's important that foreigners understand our attitude towards hierarchy. It's part of our culture and very much influences working life. We show respect to senior people and often there is a formal protocol for doing business, which may seem a little old-fashioned to some Westerners. Employees are often treated a bit like children and therefore may not be encouraged to take the initiative. They will look to the boss to give the go-ahead and also approval for their work.*

A: *And what about the family?*

B: *Yes, that's key to understanding how we do business. Many Indian companies are family-owned and the key jobs are only given to family members. Trust is very important in business and in India it is based on long-term relationships. So a foreign business person must give time to develop these relationships and understand that many doors will open and many obstacles will be removed, once you've won the trust of your partner.*

F Play the audio more than once if necessary to allow students enough time to write their notes. After playing it, let students compare their notes with a partner. Finally, check answers in class.

KEY

Use the audio script to check your answers.

G In a monocultural class, ask students to do the exercise as indicated. In a multicultural class, pair up students from different cultures and ask them to write questions for each other. Set a time limit for writing the questions then get them to role play the interview. Circulate during the exercise, making a note of any interesting points about doing business in certain countries that can be shared with the rest of the class during feedback.

H Before embarking on this exercise, you may wish to use photocopiable materials 2.1 on page 113 as a way of introducing the topic of monochronic and polychronic cultures. Ask students to look at exercise H and do it in pairs as indicated. Can they think of any specific examples / anecdotes where time has influenced cross-border business? If they were involved, how did they feel? Give an example of one you have experienced (make one up if necessary) just to set the ball rolling.

Some ways that different attitudes to time can influence doing business with another culture:

Conflicting expectations when negotiating terms, schedules and deadlines

Contrasting perceptions of a deadline

Different perceptions of efficiency

Conflicting priorities – relationships versus tasks

I If you have a multicultural class, instruct students to do the exercise as indicated.

If you have a monolingual class, tell students to imagine that they have to brief a group of foreign expats (the rest of a small group) on their culture. Get students to present their brief and encourage the 'expats' to ask questions. The brief could be prepared as a homework exercise.

▶ FOR A READING ACTIVITY ON INDIAN CULTURAL VALUES SEE PAGE 28 OF THE WORKBOOK.

▶ REFER STUDENTS TO PAGE 152 OF THE COURSEBOOK FOR A SUMMARY OF THE POINTS COVERED IN THIS BUSINESS ACROSS CULTURES SECTION.

Checklist

Review the end of unit checklist items in the Coursebook with your students, as well as the unit word field. Add any interesting pronunciation items to the pronunciation file started in Unit 1 and review the file.

Extension activity: Sentence stress

Write up the first sentence from audio script 5.1, *This approach involves opening your own facilities or subsidiaries in a new market.* Get the class to mark in the correct sentence stress pattern with dots above the stressed words. Play the audio for this sentence and let the class check their sentence stress patterns. Ask them to repeat the sentence a few times to a partner. Explain that the stressed words carry the most important part of the message. Elicit that they *tend* to be the nouns and verbs rather than words which have a more purely grammatical function, however the emphasis can *vary* depending on the point. Refer your students back to the *engaging your audience* exercise earlier in the unit. Mention that in the next unit they will be doing a further *engaging your audience* exercise. The following sentence stress exercise will help them to create a greater impact and engage their audience more effectively. Divide the class into three groups. Ask each group to mark in the sentence stress patterns to a different paragraph of the audio individually, then check the answers with the rest of their group. Play the whole audio again as a final check, then get a student from each group to read their part of the script. Audio recording will aid review.

Model answer

This approach involves opening your own facilities or subsidiaries in a new market. The good thing about it is that all the profits you make are yours to keep – well, apart from the tax paid in the country! Of course, it has its downsides. It's an enormous gamble – you might lose vast amounts of money if you misjudge things. But, who knows, one day, you might open a plant in China!

This method is better than having an export agent in the country as the key advantage is that it allows you to get to know the market better. A disadvantage is that it can be expensive. If you want to enter a market this way, you'll need your own export manager and you have to decide whether to send someone out there or recruit someone locally. The good thing with a local person is that they know the local market and the business culture.

And this is another way of getting into a new market: the advantage is you don't have to make a massive investment. This is an arrangement that we have used in some markets where earlier sales were promising. You've got to find good local partners and make sure you get a good lawyer for the contract. The only bad thing about this is that the local guys might steal your idea and then make the product by themselves without telling you!

6 The right look

Reading and speaking	In this section students are presented with language to describe the clothing company Zara's *unique selling proposition*, such as, *scarcity value*.
Vocabulary and speaking	Students learn a range of expressions to describe the fashion industry, such as *fabric* and *best selling items*.
Grammar	**the passive** Students use the passive structures to describe processes in the fashion industry via flowcharts.
Communication	**presentations: engaging your audience 2** Students practise using a range of phrases and techniques designed to relate to their audience in presentations.
Business across Cultures	**dress** In this section, students explore the visual clues that dress provides about a person's status and identity. Contrasting attitudes towards dress are also examined.

Introductory activity

With Coursebooks closed, explain that the module theme is *Markets* and that the theme of this unit is *The Right Look*. Elicit from the class what this unit theme title might mean. Why is it important to get the right look? Answers might include: *attractive designs which suit the customer's tastes, products which meet the consumer need*.

Write the opening statement from page 40 in a jumbled order on the board. Ask pairs to unscramble the sentence to make the correct statement. Rewrite the sentence on the board correctly. Ask a student to read out the statement with conviction!

The statement is an excellent grammar model for the use of *right* as opposed to *good*, which some students confuse in this context. Replace the *right* preceding *product, place* and *time* with *good*. Elicit that the sentence is no longer grammatically correct. Wipe part of the sentence leaving only *good product, good place, good time* on the board and, referring the class back to the section on determiners in Unit 5, elicit that these phrases should be preceded by *the indefinite article*. Elicit sentences incorporating *a good product*, etc. and get students to explain how the meaning differs with *the right product etc*. Examples might include: *The IPOD is a good product, we had a good time at the party yesterday*. Elicit that the resulting difference in meaning is that these nouns are now *one of possibly many*, rather than *the only one*.

Start-up

A Instruct the class to open their Coursebooks at page 40, and, referring to the opening statement, elicit a few examples of products which students feel have been very successfully marketed. In pairs, ask them to list all the things the company did to achieve this goal. Answers might include: *company responded to latest craze / fashion / untapped market, targeted the right consumer group*. Start up a unit word field around the phrase *successful marketing*.

Reading and speaking

A Get the class to look at the photo of a Zara store and in small groups, list all the things they know about the clothes shop chain, Zara. If they are not familiar with the store, ask them to imagine what sorts of products it sells, where it sells them and which market it sells to. Possible answers might include: *it sells fashion and fashion accessories / it is aimed at the youth market / it represents value for money fashion design*.

If your students are quite familiar with Zara, ask further questions to find out information such as: *it has fashion outlets in major cities in countries across Europe, Asia and Africa / it employs over 200 designers who produce relatively small batches of any one design to maintain a degree of exclusivity relying on the information they receive from the staff in their stores / Zara can adapt quickly to meet the needs of the local market / Zara is part of a larger retail group called Inditex which owns a number of fashion 'concept' labels*.

Find out if any of your students have shopped there and get them to tell the rest of the class what they think of Zara's products. Write up interesting ideas on the board and get the class to copy them down.

B Instruct the class to read the article and answer the questions individually. If necessary, pre-check items such as: *to defy, conventional wisdom, lightning speed, a holding company, retail brands, thrive, textile industry, to be under threat from, vertical integration, fabric, cluster, to sew, conveyor belt, batch, replenishment of stock, scarcity value, to catch the eye*. Do a class comprehension check.

KEY

1 *It studies the demands of customers in its stores.*

2 *It doesn't create demand for new trends using fashion shows.*

3 *It delivers at lightning speed (very quickly).*

4 *Inditex.*

5 *The designers are in daily contact with store managers.*

6 *They cut the fabric in-house and then send it to independently-owned firms for sewing.*

7 *Because most designs are quickly replaced with new ones.*

C Elicit the meaning of the expression USP. Point out that *unique selling point* is an alternative for this expression. Possible answer: *it makes the product different from competitors' products, which gives the company a strong marketing edge.* Get students to work in small groups to brainstorm the factors which create Zara's USP. Do a class review of ideas and add vocabulary to the unit word field around the phrase *unique selling proposition.* Get small groups to invent a slogan or phrase that could be used in Zara's advertising and ask one person from each group to explain why they chose it.

Vocabulary

A Ask students to match the expressions from the article to their meaning individually. Do a class answer check.

KEY

1e   2c   3f   4a   5b   6d   7i   8j   9g   10h

B Ask students to complete the sentences using the appropriate expression in A. Do a class answer check.

KEY

1 *replenishment of stock*

2 *Fabric*

3 *a cluster*

4 *bestselling items*

5 *Garments*

6 *conveyor belts*

7 *warehouses*

8 *in-house*

▶ FOR FURTHER READING AND VOCABULARY PRACTICE RELATING TO THE TOPIC OF DRESS, DIRECT STUDENTS TO PAGE 29 OF THE WORKBOOK.

▶ VOCABULARY REVIEW AND DEVELOPMENT, PAGE 60 OF THE COURSEBOOK, CAN BE DONE AT THIS STAGE.

Speaking

A Read through the instruction with the class, focusing on the sequencing language. Ask students to rearrange the boxes in the diagram to create a flow chart of Zara's design, production and delivery process individually. Get students to present their flow chart to a partner. Ask one student to present their flow chart to the class. Ask them to pay attention to intonation and pausing on the sequencing words, to make understanding clearer for the listener.

B Ask students to draw a flow chart to show how the products or services of their organisation are produced and distributed individually, and explain it to their partner.

Get a couple of students to present their flow charts to the class and do a final review of sequencing language. Add useful phrases to the unit word field.

Grammar

The passive

A Refer the class back to the flow charts they presented and elicit examples they used of the passive forms. Read through the information relating to passives with the class. Ask pairs to look at the text again on page 40 and do the exercise as instructed in the Coursebook. Do a class answer check. Elicit that the reason for using the passive here is because it is the *process* (not the doer) which is the focus of the sentence. Passives generally describe procedures and processes.

KEY

1 *In paragraph four, Fabric is cut in-house and (is) then sent to a cluster of ... and ... it is ironed, (is) carefully checked and (is) wrapped in plastic... are two examples of the passive where the verb be is omitted. This is because it can be understood to be the same as in the previous verb group. Tell students this is called ellipsis.*

2 *In paragraph four, (is) carefully checked ... and in paragraph five, Production is deliberately carried out in small batches ... are examples of passive structures with adverbs. Elicit from students that these are often placed between the auxiliary verb be and the main verb.*

3 *Paragraph five contains a modal verb, or can be found at another Zara store ...*

4 *Remind students that the subject of the passive clauses is the person or object affected by the action and that when they change passive structures to active structures they have to find a new subject, i.e. the person or thing responsible for the action. In the example most lines are replaced quickly, they'd need to invent a subject, for example Zara's managers replace most lines quickly. The writer probably doesn't know exactly who is responsible for replacing the lines, or consider that the reader needs to know this specifically.*

In the case of when the finished product is returned, it is ironed, carefully checked and wrapped in plastic ..., again the writer is focusing on the steps in the process of finishing and packaging the product attractively rather than on the workers responsible for doing it (it is obvious that Zara's various workers are responsible).

B Ask students to complete the sentences using the passive form of the verb in brackets individually and do a class check of answers.

KEY

1 *is set*

2 *is sent*

3 *can be bought*

4 *is worn*

C Ask students to do the exercise as instructed in the Coursebook.

Model answer

What happens first is that a stunning outfit is worn at a special event by a celebrity – a pop star or an actor. Next, a team of designers is sent to copy and distribute the design at lightning speed. After that, the production process is rapidly set in motion, controlled by Zara's head office in

Spain. After as little as five weeks, the outfit can be bought at Zara outlets all over the world.

Extension activity: Ask students to revise their flow charts from the previous section, using a variety of (only) passive forms. They should read them out to the class as a grammar review.

▶ FOR FURTHER INFORMATION ON THE PASSIVE, REFER STUDENTS TO GRAMMAR OVERVIEW, PAGE 158 OF THE COURSEBOOK.

▶ FOR SELF-STUDY EXERCISES ON THE PASSIVE, SEE PAGE 31 OF THE WORKBOOK.

▶ GRAMMAR REVIEW AND DEVELOPMENT, PAGE 61 OF THE COURSEBOOK, CAN BE DONE AT THIS STAGE.

Information exchange

A Ask the class if they know the fashion chain H&M. Find out what students know about it. Answers might include: *high-street fashion chain for young people / value for money like Zara, use famous designers like Stella McCartney and celebrities such as Madonna to design their clothes.* Get the class to work in groups of three to exchange information about the two companies' business strategies.

B Ask groups to work together, using A's completed chart to produce a short presentation summarising the information. Each student should take one part of it. They should use both active and passive structures in their presentation, appropriately. Review the fact that passive structures are often used when the process is more important than the person doing the process. Appoint observers to make notes on: the correct use of the passive structures, sequencing language such as *first, next, finally*, and pausing in the right places, to help the listener understand the information more clearly. Do a quick class review after each presentation.

Extension activity: Divide the class into small groups. Explain that each group is a small fashion house which survived its initial set-up and has been expanding slowly but steadily for the last five years. The fashion house is still relatively small, however, and is looking for the investment finance it needs in order to expand. Each group will have to make a presentation to a group of potential financial backers. They might even consider a takeover by a larger fashion group, like Inditex, which owns Zara. Several potential backers have already reviewed the company accounts and are satisfied that the company is in good financial health. Therefore, details about these are not needed in this presentation. They are now keen to proceed to the second step and hear more about how the company works.

Each fashion house should be prepared to explain its company structure and sell the main advantages of its current fashion concept / marketing and pricing strategy / design and production processes. Before the groups embark on their presentation preparation, ask them to brainstorm a list of key items of information they should include in it. Do a class feedback session and write up all their ideas. Get the class to copy down the full final list. Answers might include items such as: *location / ownership / direction / departmental structure / responsibilities of senior employees / number of employees / number of factories / number of retail outlets / other sales channels such as catalogue or online shopping / where and how the products are designed / by whom / how quickly these designs are turned into finished articles / the production and distribution process / marketing concept / main customer base / age range / typical price ranges.*

Next, allow the groups time to 'create' their own company using these guidelines. Move around the groups, providing help where necessary. Before asking them to start their presentation preparation, point out that the presentation should include a variety of active forms and passive forms. Elicit the fact that passive forms are appropriate when describing some aspects of companies such as where they are located, but the art of making an effective *sales pitch* is in being dynamic. Therefore, students should use active forms whenever they particularly want to achieve this effect. Contrast between the two forms is necessary. Write up: *International Sales are driven by Renate Lenke / Renate Lenke drives International Sales!* Elicit that the second version in the active form is more exciting and more likely to sell Renate as a dynamic sales director.

Finally, give each group time to prepare their presentation. Ask them to keep the presentation to a maximum of 15 minutes. They could divide it up, different students preparing and delivering different parts. This could be done as a homework activity and reviewed individually by yourself before the presentations are given. Explain that the other groups have to act as potential backers, making notes about each company during its presentation, which they should use to choose the fashion house they wish to back when all the presentations have been made.

After all the presentations have been delivered, ask each group to act as the potential financial backers. Give them ten minutes to discuss and decide on the fashion house they would be prepared to invest in. Get each group to give their verdict and explain the reasons for their final decision to the fashion houses.

Communication

Presentations: Engaging your audience 2

With Coursebooks closed, briefly review the items learnt in the previous communication section as a lead-in to this one. Elicit the ways in which the presenter can engage the audience, such as *relating the subject to the audience, showing understanding of their situation, including specific references to their needs, asking the audience a question, etc.*

A AUDIO **6.1** Read through the opening statement with the class. Check students' understanding of *reporting line*. Tell them to listen to the extract of an international food company Marketing and Sales Director and make notes on the old department structure and the plan for a new structure he is trying to sell. Do a quick class answer check, and review any new vocabulary.

KEY

	Old structure	*New structure*
Reporting line	*to the local market head*	*to the regional marketing head*
Marketing plans	*local marketing plans*	*regional marketing plans*
Performance pay	*achievement of local targets*	*achievement of regional targets*

B Ask the class to look at the Key language box. Get students to practise the language items in pairs and ask one pair to read them out. Focus on appropriate intonation *(enthusiastic for recognising success, sympathetic for acknowledging anxieties, etc.)*. Get students to listen again and write down the expressions he uses which are equivalent to the ones in the box. If necessary, do a third listening and use the audio script on page 118. Do a class comprehension check.

KEY

Use the audio script to check your answers.

AUDIO SCRIPT

So, thanks for giving up some of your time today to listen to me. I know this is a busy time of the month, so I won't keep you long. Now, I guess you've heard the rumours that we're going to be reorganising the sales and marketing function. In fact, in some markets, we've already done so. But, before we do anything here, I just wanted to take you through the arguments. This is a very successful market and that is largely down to your commitment and competence, so we want to show how we feel this change will enhance your results.

At the moment, you report direct to your Local Market Head, José Antonio, and he's been doing a fantastic job. He's now moving to a new post and in the future you'll be reporting to the Regional Market Head. The key reason for this change is that we need to maximise sales of some of our regional and global brands. We feel they're not achieving the sort of results we could expect.

Moving on, you've been doing a great job in your own local market so we want to use some of that expertise in other areas of the region. This'll mean putting together regional rather than local marketing plans. I can see some of you are looking worried. Please don't. You will still work on your sales forecasts locally but these will be integrated into a regional plan.

We also believe that you can contribute a lot to enhancing our regional results. We'll be organising the region on a project basis and we expect you to lead some of these projects. We need to make sure your local best practice is exported to some of the other markets.

I guess you'll be wondering how your pay will be affected by these changes. Currently you have some of your pay linked to achievement of your local targets. In the new structure it will be linked to regional results, but this is an opportunity for you to really influence these results.

C Read the text with the class. Divide the class into two groups. Get Group A to brainstorm a list of potential employee reactions to this change. Answers might include: *unsociable hours, disruption to family, no rise in pay*. Get Group B to brainstorm a list of likely employer's reasons for this change. Answers might include: *increasingly competitive market, need to cut costs*. Do a class review of answers. Write up all ideas and allow some time for discussion, letting groups contribute ideas to each other's lists.

Divide the class into small groups. Each person in a group should be responsible for one of the stages of the pitch, and should use the target language in exercise B and the audio script. Get groups to make their presentations to the rest of the class, with the audience noting down the target language or functions expressed. Audio or video recording

would add an element of fun and aid review. The Presentation Feedback framework on page 123 can be used.

▶ FOR DEVELOPMENT AND CONSOLIDATION OF THE LANGUAGE ABOVE, SEE PAGE 32 OF THE WORKBOOK.

▶ REFER STUDENTS TO PAGE 149 OF THE COURSEBOOK FOR A SUMMARY OF THE POINTS COVERED IN THIS COMMUNICATION SECTION.

Business across Cultures

Dress

If you have a multicultural class, ask students to find images of their national costume and prepare a two-minute presentation on the history behind the costume and any symbolism that is incorporated into it. Give them plenty of warning (about one week in advance of the lesson). When students present their costumes, invite comments and questions from the audience. Are there any similarities between the different costumes? What do the costumes tell us about the culture? Read the introduction together then ask students: *Do you judge people by their dress?*

A Turn students' attention to the photos which show people from different cultures in different types of dress. Divide the class into small groups and ask them to study the photos and work out a character profile of the individuals in the photos, using the prompts. Allow the groups about 10 minutes to create their profiles then ask each group to take it in turns to describe one individual. Can the other groups guess which person they are describing? Did they create a similar profile for that person? What helped them 'place' the person? If you have a multicultural class, are there any differences in perception?

B Instruct students to do the exercise as indicated in the Coursebook. If you have a multicultural class, get students of different nationalities to work together and ask them to make a note of any similarities or differences that they identify. Get students to briefly summarise their discussions afterwards. Care should be taken to use language which is purely observational and non-judgemental. It would be useful to mention that the differences we notice in other cultures' attitudes often reveal more about our own attitudes which we might previously have regarded as the 'norm'.

C Before reading the introduction, ask students to look at the proverb. Do they agree with it? Why? Why not?

When students have read the text individually, check understanding then ask them to answer the question *What's your view about people who pay a lot of attention to …?*

You could also ask students if they have ever experienced difficulties themselves as a result of dress when doing business in other cultures.

D [AUDIO **6.2**] Read the instructions and check understanding of the heading *dress-down culture*. It may be necessary to play the audio more than once to give students enough time to make notes under each heading. Give them time to compare their answers in pairs before checking them in class.

KEY

Use the audio script to check your answers.

AUDIO SCRIPT

Dolores: *So what clothes should I bring when I come to the UK?*

Kate: *Well, for a start, there's the weather to think of. You really need two wardrobes – one for the winter and the other for the summer. You'll need some smart clothes for the office, of course.*

Dolores: *What do you mean by 'smart'?*

Kate: *Well you know, conservative colours – blacks, greys – skirts, not too short mind and some blouses and maybe a trouser suit.*

Dolores: *It sounds a bit boring.*

Kate: *I guess it is. But some companies have started to dress down a bit – you know go a little bit more casual. The men get it wrong sometimes but I think the women still dress smartly! In some companies you may even have a dress-down or casual Friday when employees can wear what they want. Of course, this all depends on who you're going to be meeting.*

Dolores: *What do you mean?*

Kate: *Well, are you going to have much customer contact?*

Dolores: *A bit.*

Kate: *Then, I'd say play it safe! Dark colours!*

Dolores: *OK, I think I'll have to do some shopping. What about outside work?*

Kate: *That's the funny thing. A lot of people dress up in the evenings now.*

Dolores: *That's okay. So do I.*

E In a monocultural class, ask students to do the exercise as indicated. If you have a multicultural class, get students of the same nationality to work together. If that is not possible, ask individuals to prepare the briefing as a homework exercise. Get students to present their briefings in small groups made up of different nationalities.

F Ask students to read the text individually. Afterwards, check understanding by asking one student to summarise the situation in his or her own words in front of the rest of the class. Deal with vocabulary questions by asking students to provide definitions for each other. Next, ask them to discuss the questions in small groups then compare their responses in class.

G As in exercise F, ask students to read the text on their own and get one student to summarise the situation in his or her own words. Get students to discuss the issue in small groups.

H Instruct students to do the exercise in pairs. Circulate during the exercise and make a note of the language used to convey good news / bad news, to show empathy, and so on, and provide feedback on this afterwards.

Extension activity:

Ask:

What are the advantages of having a dress code?

Responses may include:

It clarifies standards.

It can prove there's no discrimination.

Then ask:

What are the disadvantages?

Responses may include:

It could be used as evidence of discrimination.

Ask small groups to create a draft of a company dress code. Get them to note the main points on flipchart paper. Set a time limit, for example, 20 minutes, then ask them to present their dress code to the rest of the class. Get them to ask questions and make comments. Can they identify any flaws in each others' codes?

For an interesting BBC article about African dress codes and an online debate dealing with the question *Is Africa's search for a formal dress futile?*, see the following website: *http://news.bbc.co.uk/1/hi/world/africa/3492932.stm*

▶ FOR FURTHER WORK ON CULTURAL ISSUES RELATING TO DRESS SEE PAGE 33 OF THE WORKBOOK.

▶ REFER STUDENTS TO PAGE 152 OF THE COURSEBOOK FOR A SUMMARY OF THE POINTS COVERED IN THIS BUSINESS ACROSS CULTURES SECTION.

Checklist

Review the end of unit checklist items in the Coursebook with your students, as well as the unit word field. Add any interesting pronunciation items to the pronunciation file started in unit 1.

Extension activity: Review the passive structures with the class, particularly the items in the key, earlier in this unit. Get small groups to brainstorm a short list of processes that they are familiar with. If necessary put a few broad ideas on the board, such as *work, study, hobbies, at home.* Student ideas might include: *preparing a meal, applying for a job, a work process such as preparing the annual report, managing a particular project, a production process, the recruitment process, sales negotiation process, preparing a presentation.* Ask each student to choose a subject and write a flow chart which they should use to present their process to the class. The flow chart could be done as a homework exercise and checked individually, before being used in the presentation.

Alternative extension activity:

Alternatively, don't ask the flow chart creators to present their own flow chart to the class. Instead, after individual checking and correction of the flow charts has been done, explain that each student is going to turn their flow chart into a passives flow chart game for the rest of the class, which will give them the opportunity to find out more about each other's jobs / interests and provide a valuable vocabulary building opportunity.

First, ask each student to convert the passive verbs in their flow chart back to their active base form. Then, get them to divide their flow chart into language chunks as in the example below.

The amount on each invoice / compare with / the amount / state on the corresponding purchase order.

If they find to be / the same / the invoice / send to the payments department.

Check these individually. Next, give each student a set of blank cards and ask them to write each language chunk onto a different card. This could be done as a homework activity if classroom time is short. Divide the class into pairs. Ask each pair to reconstruct their partner's flow chart, ordering the cards in the correct sequence. They should check and clarify any new or specialist vocabulary with their partner, if the subject matter is unfamiliar. Next, they should check that the sequence is correct with their partner. Encourage them to ask more detailed questions about their partner's process, such as:

Question: So the amount on each invoice is compared with the amount stated on the corresponding purchase order. What happens if these amounts are found to be different?

Answer: The technical services department is contacted and an explanation as to why the final cost of the spare part repair differs from the original estimate stated on the purchase order is obtained.

Question: Why might these figures be different?

Answer: Well, because the amount on the purchase order is estimated before the spare part repair is started, so obviously more serious problems might actually be discovered while the repairs are being carried out. As a result, the cost of repair could have increased substantially by the end of the service.

Finally on a piece of paper, they should then note down their partner's name and number the verbs in the flow chart, writing them down in their correct passive form. It would also be useful for them to note down any other interesting information they have learnt through questioning their partner about the process described in their flow chart. When both students in each pair have had enough time to find out as much information as possible and make appropriate notes, ask the class to jumble up their flow charts. Then, ask one person from each pair to visit another person in the class and repeat the process with their flow chart. Repeat the process as many times as you feel is productive. Then, ask the students who have been moving around the class to return to their flow charts. Ask the students who have been answering questions about their flow charts to move around the class, reconstructing / asking further questions etc.

In an open class exercise, elicit as much information as possible about each student's flow chart from the class. Write up any useful new vocabulary. Don't forget to keep your students' cards for future use!

Final activity: Intonation of delivery

Ask the class to listen to audio 6.1 again to familiarise themselves with the script. Write up the first two sentences on the board and ask the class to mark in rising, falling and flat tones, with arrows. Play the audio to check if they are correct. Ask pairs to practise delivering those lines, using the intonation marks as a guide. Some nationalities may find the degree of variation in pitch rather unnatural and somewhat comical. For them it can take a bit of getting used to! Divide the class into three groups. Choose a paragraph from audio 6.1. Ask one group to mark the audio script where they might expect to hear rising intonation, another group falling intonation, and the other group flat intonation. Play the audio as many times as necessary so students can check their answers. Next, ask students to form themselves into groups of three or more with at least one person from each of the original groups. Ask them to compare audio script markings and to prepare a final version to deliver. Then get pairs to read the paragraph to each other and get one or two students to deliver their audio script paragraph to the class. Check the intonation of the students' delivery against the original audio version. Finally, get the class to comment on the meaning of different intonation patterns, as they appear in the script, such as: showing enthusiasm, empathising with the audience, emphasising an interesting fact, rounding off a sentence.

7 Brand strategy

Reading and speaking	Students read a passage about famous brands and discuss the dangers of diversifying away from a successful strategy.
Listening	In this section, students listen to four consumers comparing local and global brands.
Grammar	**Making comparisons** Students use a range of modifying phrases to make more accurate comparisons such as, *slightly* and *nowhere near*.
Communication	**Interviewing** In this section students learn key language for effective interviewing.
Business cross Cultures	**Branding nations** Students examine the reasons for branding nations and how this is done. They also consider how they would 'brand' their own nation.

Introductory activity

With Coursebooks closed ask the class what their favourite brands are. Find out what products they represent and what sort of image they convey. Why do the students like them? Start up a unit word field around the word *brand strategy* with a branch for adjectives to describe *brand image*. Ideas might include: *trendy, well-designed, superior technology*. If possible, download the following article from the Internet, read it through with the class and find out if your students are familiar with any of the brands. Find out if they agree or disagree with the results of the survey and why. Elicit ideas as to why some of those brands are very unpopular. Answers might include: *poor quality, too expensive (Manchester tickets)*. Refer to the 'emotional attachment' to brands and elicit that this does not necessarily result in corresponding sales figures. Example: *TK Maxx is cited as an example of a shop which was described as 'most hated' as a brand but often shopped in.*
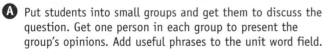
http://business.guardian.co.uk/story/0,,1776639,00.html

Start-up

Instruct the class to open their Coursebooks at page 46. Read through the opening quotation with the class and ask them if they agree with it. Find out if they think that brand image extends to the consumer. If so what do certain brands say about those who buy them? Add useful ideas to the unit word field around the word *consumers*.

A Put students into small groups and get them to discuss the question. Get one person in each group to present the group's opinions. Add useful phrases to the unit word field.

B Ask pairs to discuss their ideas with a partner. Add categories for positive and negative aspects of branding to the unit word field and write up all useful phrases which might include the following: *guaranteed quality, rip-off, buying into an image, poor value for money*.

Reading and speaking

A Elicit examples of where well-known brands have diversified from their original products to encompass a wider range of goods and/or services. Find out where this has not been

very successful. Elicit the benefits and risks of such a strategy. Answers might include: *lack of expertise, failure of certain product/service damages the image of other products/services in the range, similar type of product/customer, logical extension of range, increased profit, not enough experience of market, didn't understand customer needs well enough, incurred unexpected costs, spread focus too wide, lost profitability*

B Ask the class to read the article and match the words in italics with the definitions individually. Do a quick answer check.

KEY

1 in limbo   *2 tarnish*   *3 iconic*   *4 trimmed*
5 triggered thoughts of   *6 leverage*   *7 Re-orchestrating*

C Get students to read the article again and do the exercise as instructed in the Coursebook. Do a class comprehension check.

KEY

1 Piano

2 President and CEO of Steinway & Sons

3 Mid-level piano

4 Entry-level piano

5 Major area of future growth

D Divide the class into small groups and ask each group to brainstorm a list of advantages and disadvantages of these examples of brand extension. They should report back to the class on whether they think these examples of brand extension are a good marketing idea or not, giving their reasons. Answers might include: *customers buying smaller car like association with luxury car brand / saloon car customers feel that the image of their car brand has been downgraded and lose loyalty, long-haul travellers not attracted to cheap image of company / short-haul customers start taking long-haul holidays and profits increase,* *transatlantic airline appeals to younger customers and is a great success.* Allow time for class discussion.

E Elicit which products these brands are most famous for and write them up on the board. *Shell: oil, chemicals, gas, Rolex: watches, Nokia: mobile phones, Adidas: sportswear and equipment, Wrigley: sweets and confectionery.* Ask pairs to discuss and suggest how the brands in the exercise could be extended. Answers might include: *Shell: other forms of energy, Rolex: jewellery and fashion, Nokia: electronics, Wrigley: crisps and snacks.* Some of these companies may have diversified into areas such as these by now! If students are aware of such changes, give them time to explain their ideas.

Allow time for class discussion. Add all useful language to the unit word field.

▶ FOR FURTHER READING AND VOCABULARY PRACTICE RELATING TO THE TOPIC OF BRAND STRATEGY, DIRECT STUDENTS TO PAGE 34 OF THE WORKBOOK.

Listening

A AUDIO **7.1** Tell the class they are going to listen to four consumers comparing local and global brands. Students should do the exercise as instructed in the Coursebook individually. Do a class answer check.

KEY

1 *Market relevance*

2 *Community*

3 *Quality and standards*

4 *Social responsibility*

B Ask them to listen again and decide if the sentences are true or false.

Do a quick class comprehension check.

KEY

1 F *Global mobile-phone companies made fun of the handsets offered by TCL, a Chinese manufacturer.*

2 F *They have different tastes.*

3 F *She also relishes the experience.*

4 T

5 T

6 F *It would have affected his warranty.*

7 T

8 F *Both local and global brands should act with integrity.*

AUDIO SCRIPT

1

Obviously local brands are built with a much greater insight into what people want and need. I remember a funny situation a few years ago when global mobile-phone companies in China really made fun of the handsets offered by TCL, a Chinese manufacturer. The designs were not to Western taste, you see? But the Chinese loved them – you know, they were flashy with diamonds and things. Now TCL has passed Siemens and Samsung to become China's third-largest handset vendor after Motorola and Nokia. Ironically, Motorola itself started copying those handsets – the ones they had scorned! TCL had a far better understanding of Chinese tastes.

2

Well, when it comes to buying food, I prefer to buy local. I tend to go to my local farmers' market, not just because I believe importing and transporting food is harming the environment, but because I relish the experience. I've found farmers' markets in virtually every country I've been to. I used to go to the local souk while living in Saudi Arabia. Half the fun of it is just going in and looking around ... You meet a lot of really wonderful people and you get to support local producers. It's just not the same when you go to a big supermarket to pick up your Philadelphia cream cheese or Del Monte canned vegetables – even if they are organic! It's anonymous and it's nowhere near as enjoyable!

3

A: *Without a doubt, global brands are infinitely superior. I always buy big brand PCs – that's by far the most sensible thing to do. And I've never encountered a local PC maker who can provide after-sales support as efficiently as a large company. They can't afford to!*

B: *Hah, you must be joking! I bought my PC at a local computer store that sells its own brands and they are very well-made. If there's a problem, the vendor comes and fixes it at once. In contrast, the last time I called one of these global brands, they contacted a local repair centre who took two days to call me and then it didn't have the component in stock so I had to wait another week. Can you believe it? I could've fixed it myself in ten minutes. But, of course, that would've affected my warranty ...*

4

I always try to shop with a clear conscience whatever the brand or product. I don't like brands which use child labour to produce goods at low cost and then sell them at inflated prices in order to make more profit. Generally, people won't stand for global players exploiting employees. However, they turn a blind eye when local companies act in the same way. Big brands are under considerably more pressure to act responsibly. But, essentially, it's the same for both local and global brands: do what you do, but do it well and in an ethical way. Then customers will respect you and reward you with their custom.

C Ask pairs to discuss the question and present their ideas to the class. Write up all useful vocabulary.

Information exchange

A Read the information on Spruce Shirts with the class. Students should then do the exercise as indicated in the Coursebook. Remind students to use active listening techniques they studied on page 13 to check and clarify all of the information.

B Divide the class into small groups. Tell each group to review the collated information about Spruce Shirts and then hold a short management meeting to work out how to improve the brand's image. Appoint one person in each group to act as chairperson and another to record the main arguments and final decisions in the meeting. Circulate whilst the meetings are in progress, noting down any useful specific meetings expressions or vocabulary items, or learning points to be reviewed. The Participation in Meetings Feedback framework on page 125 is really designed for use once the meetings communication sections have been tackled, but could be used at this stage to a certain extent.

Extension activity: Ask a third person from each group to present the group's final decisions to the rest of the class after the meeting.

Grammar
Making comparisons

A Read through the opening rules and examples with the class. Ask students to complete the table as instructed in the Coursebook individually. Do a quick class answer check.

KEY

1–3 much, by far, a great deal

4–5 a little, slightly

6 just

7 nearly

8 nowhere near

B Get the class to look at the first two listening extracts on page 118. Elicit what *local brands, TCL* and *supermarket shopping* are being compared with.

KEY

Local brands are being compared with global ones in terms of the manufacturers' insight into the market.

TCL is being compared with companies such as Siemens and Samsung in terms of understanding consumers' tastes.

Supermarket shopping is being compared with shopping at farmers' markets and souks.

Instruct students to write sentences using *as ... as* or *than* individually. Do a class check of answers.

Model answers

1 Local brands are built with a much greater insight into what people want and need than brands produced by global companies.

2 TCL had a far better understanding of Chinese tastes than global mobile-phone companies (such as Siemens and Samsung).

3 Supermarket shopping is nowhere near as enjoyable as shopping locally.

C Ask pairs to write a couple of sentences for each pair of items in the exercise, using different comparative structures. Do a class check of sentences and invite students to correct each other.

D Elicit a few brand names for each of the items in the exercise, and adjectives to describe them briefly, without making any comparison with other products. Get pairs to do the exercise as indicated in the Coursebook. Ask each pair to report their discussion back to the class and encourage other students to contribute ideas and opinions.

▶ FOR FURTHER INFORMATION ON MAKING COMPARISONS, REFER STUDENTS TO GRAMMAR OVERVIEW, PAGE 159 OF THE COURSEBOOK.

▶ FOR SELF-STUDY EXERCISES ON MAKING COMPARISONS, SEE PAGE 36 OF THE WORKBOOK.

▶ GRAMMAR REVIEW AND DEVELOPMENT, PAGE 62 OF THE COURSEBOOK, CAN BE DONE AT THIS STAGE.

Communication
Interviewing

Read the opening statement with the class. Elicit key elements of answering interview questions successfully. Answers might include: *using positive language, having a confident manner, choosing appropriate language, forwarding information openly.*

A Ask a student to describe a memorable interview to the class. If necessary, prompt them with questions such as: *What was the interviewer like? How did you feel during the interview? Did they make it easy for you to talk?* Get the rest of the class to ask questions to find out whether it was successful or not. Ask pairs to discuss their experience of interviews as instructed in the Coursebook. Ask one or two pairs to report their partner's experiences back to the class. Write up all useful vocabulary on the board.

B AUDIO **7.2** Ask the class to listen to the job interview and answer the questions individually. Do a class answer check. Ask them to explain their answers to question 4, giving examples from the audio. If necessary, do a second listening. Answers might include : *interviewer wasn't very welcoming at the beginning, didn't put interviewee at ease, asked questions rather abruptly, didn't really show much interest in answers, or ask interviewee to expand on them, difficult for interviewee to make a good impression, not very polite, short, somewhat negative answers, not able to expand on answers.*

KEY

1 Marketing job.

2 A business and economics degree. He's had two jobs but doesn't have any sales experience.

3 He is analytical, good at problem-solving and has good communication skills.

AUDIO SCRIPT

A: *Did you have any problems finding us?*

B: *No, it was fine. I left in plenty of time.*

A: *Good, would you like a coffee?*

B: *No I'm fine, thanks.*

A: *OK, could you start by telling me something about yourself?*

B: *Well, I'm 28. I was born in Canada but brought up in the UK. My parents moved here when I was five. I've done all my education here except for a year which I spent in the States.*

A: *Interesting. Where were you?*

B: *I was in Miami on a university exchange.*

A: *And did you like it there?*

B: *I liked the people. I don't think I could live in Miami though.*

A: *Why's that?*

B: *It's just very different.*

A: *So, what made you go into marketing?*

B: *Well I studied business and economics at university and it was the marketing side which interested me most.*

A: *So what have you learnt so far?*

B: *Umm ... What do you mean?*

A: *I mean in your two jobs so far, what have you learned about marketing. You know, what are the key factors?*

B: I see. I guess the main thing is the consumer, the end customer. I think if you understand and can reach them, you have cracked it.

A: Really. And in our business, how do you think we reach our customers?

B: I'm not sure but, looking at your website, I suppose you do a lot of indirect stuff – you know PR events, sponsorship – that sort of thing?

A: You're right. We do that but actually our sales operation is the key. Marketing identifies the targets and also prepares the ground but it's our account managers who really make the difference. Have you had any sales experience?

B: No, I haven't.

A: So, what do you think you could bring to us?

B: Well, I'm quite analytical. I think I'm good at problem-solving and also I have good communication skills. I hope my experience at Lazenbys will be of interest to you. I was working on some new marketing tools which I mentioned in my CV.

A: Yes, we saw that. So why do you want to leave Lazenbys?

B: I think it's time to move on. I think I'm ready for a new challenge.

A: Fair enough. Is there anything you'd like to ask us?

B: Yes, I'd like to find out a bit more about the job – perhaps you could tell me what a typical day is like?

C Appoint a student to read out the Key language box to the rest of the class. Elicit one or two other possible questions for each category and write them up on the board. Then ask the class to listen again and identify the types of questions the interviewer asks.

KEY

Use the audio script to check your answers.

D Elicit what the interviewee asks about. Ask pairs to brainstorm other questions one might ask an interviewer, and do a class review. Allow time for discussion and write up any useful ideas on the board.

KEY

He asks what a typical day is like.

E Ask pairs to do the exercise as instructed in the Coursebook. Get one or two pairs to role play their scenarios in front of the class and do a class review of the key language.

▶ FOR DEVELOPMENT AND CONSOLIDATION OF THE LANGUAGE ABOVE, SEE PAGE 37 OF THE WORKBOOK.

▶ REFER STUDENTS TO PAGE 149 OF THE COURSEBOOK FOR A SUMMARY OF THE POINTS COVERED IN THIS COMMUNICATION SECTION.

Business across Cultures

Branding nations

With Coursebooks closed, tell the students that the title of this Business across Cultures section is *Branding Nations*. Can they guess what it means? Why might a nation want to 'brand' itself?

Some possible responses:

To eliminate a negative stereotype of the nation.

You may need to elicit 'stereotype' and its definition. Stereotypes can be both positive and negative, but they are often prejudicial and over-simplified. Ask for one or two examples to illustrate. For example, the British male stereotype dresses conservatively, wears a bowler hat and carries an umbrella.

To make the nation's reputation work for it rather than against it.

To boost international trade and attract investors.

To promote its culture and heritage to attract tourists.

To gain political advantage.

Then, ask students how could this be done?

Some possible responses:

Have a clear vision of what the country stands for.

Understand target markets overseas.

Sell the idea at home before presenting it abroad.

Encouraging its people to become brand ambassadors.

Involve all stakeholders, such as government bodies, the police, businesses, national heritage organisations, airlines, and others in working towards the right image.

Cultivate international press.

Achieve the right foreign and domestic policy.

Launch an advertising campaign that paints the right image.

Logos, symbols and motifs that promote the nation's unique qualities and values.

Instruct students to open the Coursebook at page 50 and read the introduction in class.

A AUDIO **7.3** Read the instructions and questions together. Play the audio more than once if necessary to allow students time to write their notes. Let students compare their notes with a partner then check answers in class.

KEY

1 *Because they think that nations are being treated in the same way as products.*

2 *He mentions Japan (technology, expensive), Britain (posh, boring, old-fashioned), Switzerland (clean and hygienic) and Sweden (Switzerland with sex appeal).*

AUDIO SCRIPT

A: *Mr Anholt, you work as a consultant to numerous governments, including Britain's. I suppose not everybody is in favour of nation branding?*

B: *You're right. At first there is often outrage. People say: 'You're treating nations like nothing more than products in the global supermarket!' But in fact, most big countries already have brands – gut associations that people make when they hear a country's name. Japan? Technology, expensive ... Britain? Posh, boring, old-fashioned. Switzerland? Clean and hygienic. Sweden? Switzerland with sex appeal. My job is to make sure these associations are a help, not a hindrance. This is fundamentally not a marketing trick. It's national identity in the service of enhanced competitiveness.*

B If possible, get students of the same nationality to work in small groups on this exercise. Instruct them to brainstorm associations on flipchart paper then briefly present their ideas to the rest of the class. Ask the other students to ask questions and make comments. Do they agree with the associations? Are there any that they would add? At this stage, ensure that purely observational and non-judgemental language is used.

C Ask one or two students to read the text out loud in class. Check understanding of words such as *backwater* and *hip*. Draw attention to the campaign's Joan Miró symbol behind the text which was used during the 1992 Barcelona Olympics. Once again, if possible, ask students to discuss the question in small groups consisting of the same nationality then get them to share their ideas with the rest of the class.

D Ask students to read the text individually then ask one or two students to summarise it in their own words in front of the rest of the class. Get students to answer questions 1 and 2 in pairs and then compare answers in class. Question 3 could be set as homework to allow students to do a little research if necessary.

KEY

1 It has an impressive market share in the US and manufactures high quality goods.

E Allow a short time for this then discuss answers in class. Remind students that stereotypes do not always reflect reality but are common perceptions based on a lack of knowledge about a country and its people. Allow a short time for this then discuss answers in class.

Possible responses:

Stereotypes of developing countries:

The country

War and conflict

Poor infrastructure

Unsanitary conditions

Famine

Corrupt governments

Low-quality goods and products

The people

Helpless

Poverty-stricken

Unskilled

Illiterate

Dependent on foreign aid

F AUDIO **7.4** Read the instructions and questions together. Play the audio and allow the students to compare their answers with a partner. Do a quick answer check.

KEY

1 If the country has a bad image, countries won't want to invest there.

2 It is about informing people about good things going on in a country to broaden and deepen their understanding of the country.

3 Yes. There have been big improvements in the skills, the infrastructure, the government and the business environment.

AUDIO SCRIPT

A: *How does nation branding help developing countries?*

B: *I think it helps a lot. The reality is that many emerging countries are fighting against a reputation – a brand image – which prevents real economic development from getting started.*

A: *What do you mean exactly?*

B: *Well, if a country is perceived as war-torn, famine-ridden, poverty-stricken, corrupt and utterly dependent on foreign aid, nobody is very likely to think of investing there, buying its products, going on holiday or going to work there. Sooner or later, the country's economy needs to get started – and that's when its negative brand gets in the way.*

A: *So, you have to change the image?*

B: *Brand strategy isn't about pretending everything's fine when it isn't, and it certainly isn't about switching off the supply of aid. But it is about helping tourists, investors and consumers learn about the good things that are going on there, to broaden and deepen their understanding of the country. It's about telling the story of the talent and the opportunity that the country has got, and giving it a chance to prosper in the global marketplace.*

A: *And are these stories being told?*

B: *Many developing countries are progressing faster than the eye can see, or certainly faster than their reputation can keep up with. There have been big improvements in the skills, the infrastructure, the government and the business environment in many of the 'transition' economies. If left to the natural course of events, these countries' reputations could take decades to catch up.*

G Before reading, refer to the Malaysian images and ask students if they recognise any of them (Petronas towers in Kuala Lumpur, new airport, Jimmy Choo shoes and Michelle Yeoh). Ask two students to read the text out loud in class. Afterwards, get students to provide definitions of words for each other. Finally, ask: *What is Malaysia's brand vision? Which companies and personalities are its brand ambassadors?*

H Ask students to do the exercise as indicated in the Coursebook. If possible, get students of the same nationality to prepare a presentation of their ideas to be presented to the rest of the class. If that is not possible, ask students to prepare it individually for homework. They should then present their ideas within small groups. Encourage other students to ask questions and make comments.

▶ FOR SELF-STUDY ACTIVITIES ON NATION BRANDING SEE PAGE 38 OF THE WORKBOOK.

▶ REFER STUDENTS TO PAGE 152 OF THE COURSEBOOK FOR A SUMMARY OF THE POINTS COVERED IN THIS BUSINESS ACROSS CULTURES SECTION.

Checklist

Review the end of unit checklist items in the Coursebook with your students, as well as the unit word field. Add any interesting pronunciation items to the pronunciation file started in Unit 1.

Final activity: Non verbal communication

Review the unit items on effective interviewing / being interviewed with the class. Establish that open questions, showing interest, etc. are an important part of the interviewer's role. Equally, willingness to forward information shows a positive attitude on the part of interviewees. Elicit that at voice level, using rising tones to indicate interest for example is often a positive behaviour, and using only flat tones could be interpreted as lack of interest or boredom.

Now remind the class that body language is an equally important part of the message we send. Divide the class into two groups. Ask one group to brainstorm a list of negative body language interview behaviours, such as *folded arms, avoiding eye contact,* and the other group to brainstorm a list of positive body language behaviours such as, *smiling, eye contact, relaxed open posture*. Do a class review of answers and allow time for discussion, especially if you have different cultures in the class with varying attitudes to positive or acceptable body language.

Ask several pairs to redo the interviews in exercise E, using very closed body language. Appoint a couple of observers to each pair. They should report back on the impression their student gave, describing their body language and how it influenced the interview. Elicit from students how easy it was to use the key language items from the communication exercise effectively with closed or negative body language.

Repeat the process with different pairs who should now use more positive body language.

8 The hard sell

Reading and speaking
In this section students encounter a number of phrases to talk about *product placement*, such as *positive association* and *mass media*.

Listening
In an interview with Antonio González, an advertising expert, students learn a variety of expressions relating to *niche market* advertising, such as *minority group* and *emotional connections*.

Grammar making predictions
Students use a range of phrases to talk about future probabilities.

Communication feedback
In this section, students explore different ways of giving feedback.

Business cross Cultures global marketing
This section highlights the advantages of local advertising. It also examines issues that have to taken into account when trying to reach a local market.

Introductory activity

Before the lesson, find magazine pictures advertising products and distribute in class. Ask students to think about what their picture is trying to convey. Ask questions such as: *Who is this advertisement aimed at? What is it trying to sell? What image is it trying to sell about the product or consumer? Does it work?* Get each student to show their picture to the rest of the class and to explain their answers to these questions.

Start-up

Instruct the class to open their Coursebooks at page 52. Read the opening poem with the class. Check the meaning of *billboard* and ask the class questions like: *What sort of person might have written this poem? Where might they have been?* Answers might include: *someone travelling through a large city.*

A Ask the class what ideas they think the poet is trying to express. Find out whether any of your class sympathise with the poet. Elicit opinions about the effect of advertising on your students' lives. Start up a unit word field around the word *advertising* and write up any useful language items.

B Read through the items in the box with the class and get students to do the exercise as indicated in the Coursebook. Do a class review of the pairwork discussions and add useful language items to the unit word field.

Extension activity: Ask prompt questions such as: *Which types of advertising are becoming more popular? Which are the most persuasive / sophisticated / expensive / successful / annoying / immoral?* Get each pair to discuss a different advertising medium. Then, get them to briefly report their discussions to the class. Add useful language items to the unit word field.

C Check the meaning of *niche* and *mass* before asking pairs to answer the questions. Do an opinion poll of answers. If pairs' answers differ, allow time for class debate and get students to explain their ideas and give opinions, until a consensus has been reached. Add useful language items to the unit word field.

Reading and speaking

A Read the statement with the class and ask students to do the exercise as indicated in the Coursebook. Do a class answer check.

KEY
1c
2a
3b
4d

Extension activity: Divide the class into two groups. Get one group to brainstorm a list of films, books or TV series in which product placement is visible. Prompt them to think about drinks / jewellery / clothing / gadgets, etc. Ask the other group to brainstorm a short list of films or film audiences for which they feel product placement would not be possible. It might be more useful to think more specifically about which types of product would not be suitable for certain types of audience. Answers might include: alcohol / cigarettes for children. Period films would exclude products which were not relevant in that period. Allow time for debate during a class feedback in which students should justify their lists. Add useful items to the unit word field around the phrases *ideal for product placement / unsuitable for product placement*.

Alternatively, divide the class into three groups and assign each group one of the following people: *advertisers, film producers, audiences*. Ask them to brainstorm the advantages and disadvantages of product placement for this category. Do a class review and add useful items to the unit word field around the words, *advantages* and *disadvantages*. Possible answers might include: *Advantages: film production companies can use the revenue to fund film-making, advertisers can reach a large captive audience via a big screen, products are associated with memorable films, audiences can see the product clearly. Disadvantages: film producers may have to incorporate products they don't really want in their films, be forced to make sure they are in shot for a specific length of time, lose a sense of integrity, audiences are subliminally bombarded by products they may not be able to afford, parents may not want this for their children.*

B Explain that the class are going to read an article which was published on the release of the James Bond film *Die Another Day* in 2002. Find out if anybody has seen it, where it was set and who the main supporting characters were. Get a student to summarise the plot for the rest of the class. Read the questions with the class and ask pairs to discuss them. Do a quick class feedback. Allow time for discussion. Answers might include: *increased sales / positive association with heroic figures / all age groups / likely to rise as we live in a mass media age.*

C Instruct the class to read the article. Do a quick answer check.

KEY

1 *It has become one long advert.*

2 *They can get the reach they wouldn't be able to get elsewhere.*

3 *Bond films appeal to both the young and old. The ratio of men to women is 60:40.*

4 *It won't be too long before interactive television and mobile technology link up.*

Add a category called *technological innovation* to the unit word field. Elicit and write up recent or future methods of selling products which have been 'placed' in films and TV programmes.

Extension activity: Get small groups to pick a product and to brainstorm a list of maximum five (existing) films (which for the purposes of this exercise are about to be remade) in which they, the product advertisers, will 'place' this product. Groups should briefly present their product placement idea to the class, explaining how the product would be used or displayed in these films and why these films would be appropriate vehicles for the product, in terms of image, which consumer groups the product would be targeted at, etc. Encourage the audience to act as a very commercially conscious panel which has to assess whether the films are appropriate. They should ask questions during the presentation and give their opinions. Finally, they should decide which films to accept as product placement vehicles for the product presented.

▶ VOCABULARY REVIEW AND DEVELOPMENT, PAGE 61 OF THE COURSEBOOK, CAN BE DONE AT THIS STAGE.

▶ FOR FURTHER READING AND VOCABULARY PRACTICE RELATING TO THE TOPIC OF ADVERTISING, DIRECT STUDENTS TO PAGE 39 OF THE WORKBOOK.

Listening

A Ask the class to read the quotation about mass marketing. Find out if they agree with it and encourage them to explain why. Answers might include: *global market=global mind / decreasing diversity in taste / cultural values still vary greatly.* Allow a little time for debate. Add useful items to the unit word field.

B Read the instruction with the class and ask pairs to do the exercise as indicated in the Coursebook. Elicit ideas from the group. Write up any useful ideas on the board.

C AUDIO **8.1** Tell the class to listen to the first part of the radio interview and answer the questions individually. Do a quick answer check.

KEY

1 *It is worth about $700 billion.*

2 *The slogan 'It's the network' and the motto 'For English, press two'.*

3 *Community events, sponsoring sporting and music events, and organising adult soccer tournaments.*

AUDIO SCRIPT

Interviewer:	*Welcome to Business Update. This morning I'm going to be talking to Antonio González of AG Advertising about reaching the Hispanic market. Good morning Antonio ... Now, you majored in Hispanic marketing at DePaul University and your agency deals exclusively with the Hispanic market. Why is the Hispanic market so important?*
Antonio González:	*Well, this is the biggest niche market since the baby boomers of post-war US – the generation of children who grew up with completely different expectations, attitudes and tastes from their parents. The Hispanic market is worth about $700 billion, and is expected to grow to $1 trillion over the next few years. Their disposable personal income is greater than that of any other minority group in the United States.*
Interviewer:	*So how do companies reach this market? Can you give us some examples?*
Antonio González:	*Sure. Sprint and Verizon, two wireless carriers, have used a range of tactics. One very simple example – Verizon's English slogan was 'It's the network' but that doesn't translate very well into Spanish, so they came up with conectividad total, or 'total connectivity'. You can't simply translate slogans into Spanish – that's a pitfall many advertisers get into.*
Interviewer:	*Right ...*
Antonio González:	*Then there's Movida Communications Inc., which provides wireless voice and data services and targets the Hispanic market. The company's customer service motto is: 'For English, press two.' Anyway, there are more effective ways of gaining customer loyalty. The language is only a small part of it. Verizon has used community events to form 'emotional connections' with customers. For example, it has served as an official sponsor of World Cup soccer. And it also organised adult soccer tournaments in cities with large Latino populations.*
Interviewer:	*I see ... So they're using a kind of grassroots tactic ...*

Antonio González: Exactly. Sprint uses music and entertainment to establish similar bonds with its customers. Its live Spanish-language television – Sprint TV en Vivo – was the first in the United States. And the Sprint Music Store stocks more than 20,000 Latin-related songs. What's more, the company is the title sponsor of the 2007 US tour of the Latin rock group Maná, which attracted more than 12 million people in 32 countries on its last global tour.

D AUDIO **8.2** Ask the class to listen to the second part of the interview and answer the questions individually. Do a class comprehension check.

KEY

1 They are becoming aware that Hispanics are not one homogenous group.

2 In their advertising, they try to show universal human themes that appeal to viewers regardless of language or culture.

3 Hispanics are not visible in mainstream advertising.

4 The fusion market represents Hispanics who relate to both American and Latino cultures. Antonio mentions the Toyota ad in which a father speaks to his son in Spanish and English.

AUDIO SCRIPT

Interviewer: One thing I'd really like know is – Does it make sense to have a 'Hispanic market'? I mean, it groups together people from different backgrounds and cultures. After all, what does a lawyer from Argentina, raised in a middle-class neighbourhood in Buenos Aires, for instance, have in common with a factory worker from Mexico? Besides, does a Hispanic born in the US share many similarities with a newly arrived Hispanic immigrant?

Antonio González: You're right – that's why advertisers are changing the way they advertise to this market. Most money spent on Hispanic advertising targets individuals born outside the United States, yet the majority of Hispanics in the US were born here. Many are fluent in English and Spanish, and identify strongly with both American and Latino cultures. Advertisers are becoming more aware of this and are changing their approach. They try to show universal human themes that appeal to viewers regardless of language or culture.

Interviewer: In that case, why not just use mass marketing campaigns to reach out to Hispanics?

Antonio González: Well, this group is not very visible in mainstream advertising. How many Latino faces do you see?

Interviewer: That's true ...

Antonio González: The answer is probably to treat this group as a 'fusion market', this is a term we use for bilingual and bicultural markets. Actually, a good example of advertising for the fusion market is the bilingual ad Toyota ran during the Super Bowl to promote its 2007 Camry Hybrid vehicle. You know, where a father speaks to his son in Spanish and English, reflecting the car's ability to switch from gas to electric power. I've no doubt we'll see more examples of this type of advertising in the future.

Interviewer: Indeed. Many people are convinced that Latino culture will eventually become the new mainstream popular culture. If that's the case, your experience in the Hispanic market is sure to give you a head start.

Antonio González: Well, I certainly hope so.

Interviewer: Well, thank you for joining us this morning and giving us an interesting insight into targeting the Hispanic market.

Ask the class to listen to audios 8.1 and 8.2 again for new key phrases which can be added to the unit word field, such as: *universal themes, mainstream advertising.*

E Start a class discussion on the main niche markets in your students' country or countries. Ask questions like: *Do you feel you are part of a niche market? Are there any fusion markets? How are they likely to change in the future?*

Speaking

A Read the instructions and list of products and services with the class. Divide the class into small groups and ask each group to devise an advertising campaign. Provide the class with flipchart paper for them to brainstorm their ideas. Get each group to write down a list of ways in which they will grab their niche market's attention with this product / service and ask them to present their ideas to the class. Allow time for comment and discussion. Add useful phrases to the unit word field.

Grammar
Making predictions

A Read the rules about making predictions and the model sentences with the class. Elicit degrees of certainty for each one as a class exercise.

KEY

1 certainty

2 doubt

3 probability

4 possibility

5 probability

6 certainty

B Ask pairs to do the exercise as instructed in the Coursebook. Do a quick class answer check.

KEY

1 definitely / certainly / inevitably

2 I have no / There's no

3 (absolutely) certain / sure / positive / convinced

4 sure to / bound to / certain to

C Write the numbers 10 per cent, 25 per cent and 75 per cent on the board. Ask pairs to read the the model phrases and list them under these percentages to show how probable they are. Do a quick class check. Then, get pairs to use the structures to give their own opinions about the statements in the exercise. Partners should agree or disagree and give their own opinion. Do a class review of the discussions.

D This short presentation could be prepared as a homework exercise. Audio or video recording would aid a class review. Appoint observers to note down the structures used and comment on them.

  ▶ FOR FURTHER INFORMATION ON MAKING PREDICTIONS, REFER STUDENTS TO GRAMMAR OVERVIEW, PAGE 160 OF THE COURSEBOOK.

  ▶ FOR SELF-STUDY EXERCISES ON MAKING PREDICTIONS, SEE PAGE 41 OF THE WORKBOOK.

  ▶ GRAMMAR REVIEW AND DEVELOPMENT, PAGE 62 OF THE COURSEBOOK, CAN BE DONE AT THIS STAGE.

  ▶ REFER TO PHOTOCOPIABLE 2.3 ON PAGE 117 FOR LESS CONTROLLED PRACTICE OF MAKING PREDICTIONS.

Communication

Feedback

A Read the introduction with the class. Write up some questions on the board, such as: *What type of feedback do you receive? Who is it from? Does it point out successes, show you how to develop weak points or simply state when you are wrong? How do you feel when you receive these types of feedback? Do you think it helps you?* Elicit one or two answers from the class and then ask students to discuss their own experiences in pairs.

B AUDIO **8.3** Tell students they are going to listen to a performance review session.

Read the instruction with the class and check students' understanding of the items in the table. Ask the class to listen and complete the form.

KEY

Targets	Progress	Further action?
1 Take a more active role in project work	Anna is pleased with the progress and everyone is getting on well together.	None mentioned
2 Time management	The course was fine but feels he has too much to do.	A coach

C Get feedback from the class on the questions in this exercise. Write up answers, including any phrases the class remember hearing which relate to the questions. They probably won't remember many at this stage.

KEY

She got the feedback from asking Bill a series of questions

and then expanding on his answer. The first target got affirmative feedback and the second received development feedback.

D Ask pairs to read the Key language items to each other. Then with Coursebooks briefly closed, read out a few example sentences and elicit their functions. Then ask the class to listen again and tick the phrases that they hear.

KEY

Use the audio script to check your answers.

AUDIO SCRIPT

A: *So Bill, how do you think things have gone so far, this year?*

B: *Pretty well, I think.*

A: *Good, let's have a look at your targets. I seem to remember there were two main ones. Yes, the first was to take a more active role in project work. Do you feel you are doing that?*

B: *Yes, I do. I've been making quite an effort. As you know, I've been working on the 2020 project and I feel I've made more of a contribution. I don't know. What do you think?*

A: *Well, from what I hear, it's going well and Anna seems pleased with its progress and the fact that everybody's getting on well together. So, I'm pleased about that and I can see you've made a real effort.*

B: *Great. I feel much more involved now and I really care about each project I work on.*

A: *Good. So, the other target was in terms of your time management. You went on that course and we agreed that you needed to get better at prioritising. So how's that been going?*

B: *To be honest, not very well. The course was fine but it's easy in theory. In practice, I just seem to have too many things to do.*

A: *I understand. I think we all do. But it's stressful for you and your colleagues if you are always struggling with your deadlines.*

B: *I know, I know. But it's difficult to change. Some days I feel I've got nowhere. In fact some days I feel I've gone backwards.*

A: *What's stopping you from prioritising?*

B: *I do. I make a list but then other things come up and they're not on the list. I don't know. It's just really difficult and I know it's no good for Anna and the rest of the team.*

A: *So what are you going to do?*

B: *I wondered whether I could have a coach for a few months. I've heard that some people have one. What do you think?*

E Put students into pairs and get them to do the exercise as instructed in the Coursebook. Get one or two pairs to role play in front of the class. Give affirmative and developing feedback on their performance!

  ▶ FOR DEVELOPMENT AND CONSOLIDATION OF THE LANGUAGE ABOVE, SEE PAGE 42 OF THE WORKBOOK.

  ▶ REFER STUDENTS TO PAGE 149 OF THE COURSEBOOK FOR A SUMMARY OF THE POINTS COVERED IN THIS COMMUNICATION SECTION.

  ▶ COMMUNICATION REVIEW AND DEVELOPMENT EXERCISES, PAGE 63 OF THE COURSEBOOK, CAN BE DONE AT THIS STAGE.

Business across Cultures
Global marketing

With Coursebooks closed, tell students the following anecdote:

Promoters of the World Cup sold footballs decorated with the flag of each country that qualified for the finals. Muslims were extremely offended when Saudi Arabia's flag was put on a football.

Ask the class if they can guess why Muslims were so offended.

The reason is as follows:

The name of Allah is on Saudi Arabia's flag so should never be associated with any commercial purpose and, more seriously, never be touched with the foot as the foot is considered unclean in the Middle East.

Instruct students to open their Coursebooks on page 56 and read the introduction.

A Before allowing groups to embark on the discussion, ask them what challenges the football anecdote highlighted in terms of reaching a local market. Ask students to brainstorm further issues on flipchart paper and then compare their ideas with the rest of the class.

Some issues that have to be taken into account:

Religion

Language

Taboos

Tastes

Local competition

Gender roles

Education and literacy

The most accessible forms of advertising media

B If you have a multicultural class, ask students of different nationalities to work together, comparing the ways the products would be marketed in their cultures. Each pair should then tell the class the main differences and similarities that they identified.

If you have a monolingual group, do the exercise as indicated but also ask them to try to guess how certain products would be marketed abroad.

C Ask students to do the exercise as indicated in pairs. While students are reading, circulate and help them if they have difficulty understanding their texts. Remind them to check and clarify details when they are listening to their partners as they will need the information for the next exercise.

D Tell students to imagine that they are marketing consultants giving a presentation at a seminar for marketing managers. To make it more realistic, you could ask the groups to prepare very simple slides (a maximum of three on OHP transparencies, for instance) to support their presentation. Give them between 20 and 30 minutes to prepare. Circulate during this time, helping with language issues and making a note of the language used during their preparation. They should then give their presentations to the rest of the class.

During the presentations, ask the members of the 'audience' to think of at least one question they can ask the presenters.

E AUDIO 8.4 Before looking at the exercise, ask students to define 'globalisation'. Write their definition(s) on the board.

Possible response:

Globalisation is the process of connecting the world's markets and businesses. So far, this has been done through deregulation of cross-border trade and improved communications.

Then ask students why some markets might object to globalisation.

Possible responses:

It destroys the diversity of local cultures.

It results in unfair competition for local companies.

Draw students' attention to exercise E and the table for their notes. Pre-teach some words from the audio, such as *icon* and *Anglo-Saxon*. Play the audio more than once if necessary to allow students enough time to write their notes. After playing it, let students compare their notes with a partner. Finally, check answers in class. During open class discussion, ask students what they think about how these countries resisted globalisation. Would these methods work in their own countries?

KEY

Market	How they resist globalisation	Impact
Iran	Ban advertisements for imported goods	Makes these brands more popular
France	Protect culture from	Impact not very great
Africa	Have their own brands or adapt international brands	Makes it cheaper for consumers

AUDIO SCRIPT

1

In Iran, they have recently tried to ban advertisements for imported goods. It's all part of a campaign against foreign cultural influence. There have been lots of attempts to ban icons of Western culture such as Barbie dolls and Coca-Cola. In fact, this has tended to make them even more popular – especially with the young. A couple of years ago, ads for Castrol oil showing the face of the football star David Beckham, with the slogan 'Makes your bike go like Beckham' were blacked out on the orders of the authorities and TV commercials showing his bare legs were withdrawn.

2

Here in France we have a long tradition of trying to protect our culture from Anglo-Saxon influence. The Académie Française rules on language issues and tries to protect the French language from English words such as le weekend *and* le jogging. *We also try to limit the number of American films shown in French cinemas – again we are trying to protect our own film industry. I'm not sure that the impact of these measures is very great.*

3

In most parts of Africa, they have their own brands or African versions of the brands which we have. They can't afford the prices we pay so this way, the products they sell are cheaper. Very often they buy in smaller quantities and adapt the product to their tastes. Milo, the drink made by Nestlé, is a good example. In Ghana it is mixed with hot or cold water instead of milk. In Australia, where it started, they always drink it as a milk drink. In Africa they have been developing our products and adapting yours for years.

63

F Encourage the pairs to discuss their reasons for their views. Ask students to share their views with the rest of the class.

Possible responses:

Can markets resist globalisation?

*Many people think that globalisation cannot be resisted because trade and direct investment are catalysts for economic development, industrialisation, democratisation and the improvement of domestic social conditions. There is also global demand for certain goods and services. How many countries can you visit where children don't **want** to go to McDonald's? Furthermore, greater globalisation leads to a wider choice of products which means that prices are often driven down by cheap imports.*

Many developing countries fear lagging behind the industrialised world so they are reluctant to resist globalisation.

Do you think the government should protect their local market and culture? How?

- *Establish policies and procedures that will promote sustainability of the local culture and way of life.*
- *Set up informal barriers against outside competition.*
- *Resist free trade agreements.*
- *Support and subsidise local manufacturing, agriculture, etc.*

G Read the instructions and introductory text together in class. Check that students understand what a *telecom service* is by asking someone to explain. In a multicultural class, make sure students are paired with someone of a different nationality. This will make the information exchange more challenging if they have to deal with a foreign accent. Allow students plenty of time to do steps one and two. Before embarking on step three, make sure that everyone understands the exercise: to brainstorm an advertisement for the telecom service. Tell them that they can choose to create *an outline of a TV advert* or create *a draft of an outdoor poster* (write these options on the board). Set a strict time limit for preparation and ask students to brainstorm their ideas on flipchart paper. Finally, ask students to show their ideas to the rest of the class and explain the rationale behind their campaign. Get the other students to ask questions and make comments.

- ▶ FOR FURTHER WORK ON THE TOPIC OF GLOBAL VERSUS LOCAL ADVERTISING SEE PAGE 43 OF THE WORKBOOK.
- ▶ REFER STUDENTS TO PAGE 152 OF THE COURSEBOOK FOR A SUMMARY OF THE POINTS COVERED IN THIS BUSINESS ACROSS CULTURES SECTION.

Checklist

Review the end of unit checklist items in the Coursebook with your students, as well as the unit word field. Add any interesting pronunciation items to the pronunciation file started in Unit 1.

Final activity: Briefly review the subject of final activities from the last three units in module 2, sentence stress, rising and falling tones, and body language. Get pairs to look at audio script 8.3 on page 120 again. Ask them to role play this feedback session with each other, bearing these three important elements of communication in mind. Get one or two pairs to role play to the class. Audio or video recording would aid review. Ask the class to comment on the intonation and body language displayed.

Business Scenario 2

DUA

This Business Scenario concerns a UK bicycle producer's plans to launch its bicycles on the Indian market. Building on the Business across Cultures section of Unit 5 on India, this unit deals with leisure interests in India and marketing to India's high-end young market. The speaking exercise requires students to prepare and give presentations on different aspects of the Indian market and cycling culture. This allows students to review and practise the language of presenting, which appears in Units 5 and 6. In the discussion, which acts as a warm-up for the meeting exercise afterwards, students consider which cycling products would be most suitable for the Indian market. The aim of the meeting is for participants to share their marketing ideas and decide on an appropriate marketing campaign. The writing exercise involves writing brief notes on the meeting.

Introductory activity

With Coursebooks closed, ask students:

What outdoor sports are popular in your country?

Which alternative sports are you aware of in your country?

Answers may include: *skateboarding, surfing, snowboarding, paragliding, canoeing, mountain biking, BMX stunt riding.*

How do such sports become popular? Students may answer: *through national / international sporting events, promoted by popular celebrities, campaigns targeting young people to encourage healthier lifestyles, the investment in and setting up of sporting facilities, association with youth fashion and style.*

Next, elicit the following types of bikes and their uses:

Mountain bike

Tour bike (like those used in the Tour de France)

BMX (bike for doing stunts on very rough tracks)

Street bike

Folding bike

Electric bike

Ask students: *Who would ride each one?* And: *Do you know of any big brand bicycles that are popular in your country? Which are status symbols?*

Background

Read the background together in class.

Speaking

Before looking at this exercise, tell students that they are going to give a presentation and ask them for some tips on how to engage the audience. Write their responses on the board.

Possible responses:

Tips

Make contact with the audience – Tell them something personal / Ask them a question

Keep an eye on your physical distance from the audience – Do not stand too far back / Do not stand behind a desk

Give detailed information on handouts, rather than slides

Use slides only occasionally

Get feedback from the audience throughout presentation

You could ask students to refer back to Units 5 and 6 for more presentations language.

Read the instructions then draw attention to the Useful language, asking students to try to incorporate at least three of the phrases in their presentations.

Divide the class into groups of four and then split each group into Team A and Team B. Tell students that their presentations, including the question time, should not last longer than five minutes. It would be nice if the presentations were supported with a few slides, so give each team a *maximum* of three OHP transparencies to create simple slides on. Allow around 20 minutes to prepare the presentations and go around during this time helping students where necessary.

Before they give their presentations to the rest of their team, remind the 'audience' that they should ask questions and check and clarify details because they will need the information for an exercise later. While the students are giving their presentations, circulate and make a note of their use of presentations language, visuals and the way they engage their audience. Provide corrections and feedback after the meeting.

Discussion

Before embarking on the discussion exercise, check understanding of words in the advert, such as *frame, state-of-the-art, gears, brakes, low-maintenance, trendy,* and *commute.* Ask students to discuss this in pairs for five minutes then compare their views with the rest of the class. Ensure that they give reasons for their opinions.

Meeting

Read the introduction to the exercise together. It says that Aarit Motala is going to talk about the products he has chosen for the Indian market, so tell students that they will find out whether he has chosen the same products that they chose in the previous exercise. Emphasise that the aim of the meeting is to *share marketing ideas* and *to come up with a strategy for a marketing campaign.*

Divide the class into groups of four and assign roles to each student. Ask a well-organised and reasonably confident student to play the role of Aarit Motala, who will chair the meeting.

Allow five minutes for preparation. Warn students that they will need to take notes about any decisions made during their meetings (they will need this information to do the writing exercise below). Circulate while students are preparing their roles to help with any queries concerning language or context.

Set a time limit of 20 minutes for the meeting. If you have a small group and therefore only one meeting taking place, record it on video to use during feedback. Try to use it selectively to highlight positive interaction and elicit areas that could be improved.

Writing

This could be set as homework. Ask students to decide who the notes are for before they begin writing. Correct their writing outside class then select some examples to use in class to highlight weaknesses and strengths common to the group.

Review and development 5–8

Vocabulary: Market entry

A This is best done individually or for homework.

KEY

1 construct

2 end

3 absolutely

4 raise

5 Inner

6 experiments

7 result

Grammar: Determiners and quantifiers

A Before looking at the rules in the book, put the following on the board:

Singular count	Plural count	Uncount

a   enough   any   neither   several   this
another   little   both   other   many of   much of
all of   little of   a few of

Elicit where each word should go in the table.

Next, write the following sentences on the board:

1 Few staff attended the meeting.

2 A few staff attended the meeting.

3 Few of the staff attended the meeting.

Ask students what the difference is between the sentences.

1 Negative – We're not very happy about turnout.

2 Positive – At least some were there despite their busy schedules.

3 More people were expected.

Remind students that if a quantifier is followed by 'of', the noun must be preceded with a definite article (the) or a possessive adjective (my, your, etc.). For example,

*Many **of** our colleagues*

*Much **of** the time*

Instruct students to read the rules on page 36 of the Coursebook again then ask them to do exercise A in pairs. Check answers in class.

KEY

1 Neither

2 little

3 less

4 either

5 Many of

6 few of

7 Few

Vocabulary: Production, distribution and delivery

A Ask students to do this exercise in pairs then check answers in class. If students do not understand some of the words, get other students to provide definitions.

KEY

Store large quantity of goods in a warehouse.

Carry out production in small batches.

Place an order for 1,000 components.

Ship the finished products to the customer.

Replenish stock quickly

Develop a prototype according to specifications.

Grammar: The passive

A Ask students to look at the rules and examples as a homework exercise prior to this lesson. Instruct students to do the exercise in pairs then check answers in class.

Model answers

1 First, an order for a customised tool is placed.

2 Then 'quality and production planning' is done.

3 After that, the prototype is developed based on the customer's specifications.

4 Next, a trial on the prototype is carried out to ensure that …

5 Then a production trial run is done to confirm that …

6 After that, mass production is carried out.

7 Next, the tools are inspected for any irregularities.

8 Finally, the tools are packed and shipped to the customer.

Extension activity: This is an entertaining activity for reviewing passives. Give pairs of students 16 blank strips of paper (approximately 5cm × 15cm). Demonstrate the activity by writing the following sentences or your own on much larger strips of paper (so everyone can see) prior to the lesson and get students to match the two halves: the more ambiguous the sentences the better as students can identify some absurd or humorous matches.

The computer has been	repaired.
32 workers were	made redundant.
Confidential information was	stolen from my laptop.
The robot will be	controlled by an operator.
Bill Gates was	officially knighted.
Smoking in the office has been	banned.
All staff who met their targets were	given extra holiday leave.
The first iPod was	sold six years ago.

Before students write their sentences, warn them that should begin the second slip of paper with *the past participle*, as in the examples above.

Allow up to 10 minutes for the pairs to write their sentences. While they are doing this, check that they understand the exercise and that their sentences are grammatically correct. Students should then mix up their sentences and exchange them with another pair who have to match the two halves of each sentence.

Vocabulary

A This is best done individually or for homework.

KEY

1 iconic	2 extended	3 billboard	4 niche
5 Sponsorship	6 Telemarketing	7 placement	8 fusion

Grammar: Making comparisons

Write the following on the board:

1 System A is _____?_____ more efficient than System B.
2 Candidate A _____?_____ as experienced as Candidate B.

Ask students if they can think of any words that will fit into the gaps. (See exercise A on page 48 of the Coursebook.)

Once you have elicited as many of the words as possible, turn to page 48 of the Coursebook to look at the rules again.

A Ask students to do this exercise in pairs then compare answers in class.

Model answers

Brand B is much more reliable than Brand A.

Brand B is slightly better value for money than Brand A.

Brand A's running costs are marginally more expensive than Brand B's.

Brand A is just as stylish as Brand B.

Brand A is nowhere near as easy to maintain as Brand B.

Brand A's customer service is infinitely more satisfactory than Brand B's.

Brand B's CO_2 emissions are considerably higher than Brand A's.

Brand B is a little safer than Brand A.

B This could be set as a homework exercise.

Grammar: Making predictions

A If you would like to make the exercise a little more challenging, ask students to do exercise A in pairs before looking at the rules and examples on page 54 of the Coursebook.

KEY

Certainty	Probability	Possibility	Doubt
I'm certain that ...	is / are likely ...	There's a good chance that ...	... I doubt ...
I've no doubt that ...	should ...	may / might / could ...	... is / are unlikely ...
... is / are bound to ...			

B Ask students to do the exercise in pairs then check answers in class.

Model answers

1 are likely

2 I've no doubt

3 should

4 I doubt

5 are bound

6 could

7 it's likely

Communication

You could ask students to study the Communication pages for homework prior to the lesson.

A Ask students to do this exercise in pairs then check answers in class.

KEY

1d	2b	3f	4e	5a	6c

B Ask students to do this exercise in pairs then check answers in class.

KEY

1 faced   2 contribute   3 background   4 career
5 finding   6 join   7 add

C Ask students to do this exercise in pairs then check answers in class.

KEY

1 Could you tell me about your targets?

2 I can see you have made a big effort.

3 I feel I am going backwards.

4 What is getting in your way?

5 How is it going?

6 I think I am on the right track.

7 I am finding it very difficult.

Money

MODULE OVERVIEW

AIMS AND OBJECTIVES

The themes in this module reflect the subject of money, and include the discussion of emerging private sector markets, such as China, the pros and cons of investing in such markets, improving company finances, and getting third world countries out of the poverty trap. A number of grammar and vocabulary items are reviewed and practised in the context of 'money'. Students practise using appropriate conjunctions and linkers, to express cause and effect, become more familiar with referring and sequencing language and develop their use of multi-word prepositions commonly used in a business context. The communication sections focus on leading and participating in meetings and aspects of negotiating, such as bargaining and conflict resolution. The Business across Cultures section in this module provides students with an insight into the cultural values and assumptions of a different culture: China, Russia, Brazil and Africa. A broad range of cultural concepts feature in this module; for instance, the concept of 'face', expressing emotion, and attitudes towards rules and regulations.

At the end of the module, students should be able to:

- discuss the subjects of emerging overseas markets, cross-border mergers and other forms of overseas direct investment, improving profitability, and pulling third world countries out of the poverty trap

- use appropriate conjunctions and linkers, to express cause and effect

- be conversant with referring and sequencing language such as *this* and *that*

- use a range of multi-word prepositions commonly used in a business context

- report speech using a range of verbs

- lead meetings more effectively, managing the four Ps: *preparation, purpose, process* and *people.*

- become more interactive in meetings

- use a range of expressions to bargain more successfully

- employ strategies for conflict resolution

- recognise and understand some key concepts of Chinese, Russian, Brazilian and African culture

THEMATIC OVERVIEW

This module provides an insight into current issues connected with the now well-established idea of a global market. Globalised industrial giants need to display evidence of corporate social responsibility, particularly when making use of resources in third world countries, or emerging economies, for their own gain. How closely to invest in such markets, or more specifically, exactly what type of investment to make, is a tricky decision. Poor infrastructure and social and political instability have to be considered. When cutbacks have to be made, what is the least damaging way to do this? Can cutbacks be avoided by exploring new markets and boosting the profit margin on work already done?

MAIN AUDIO CONTENTS

UNIT 9: an extract of an economist talking about the growth of the Chinese economy; extracts from a business meeting whose leader is managing the four Ps; a businessman talks about his experience of doing business in China.

UNIT 10: an interview with a specialist in country risk analysis, extracts from a meeting containing several types of questions.

UNIT 11: an extract of a speaker talking about a conference budget; four extracts of negotiations; an interview with Maria Fernandes about work and social life in Brazil.

UNIT 12: an interview with Sanjay Chakraborty, a specialist in poverty reduction, in two parts; 10 statements to be turned into reported speech; a dialogue of a conflict; a representative of a Swedish aid agency talks about the problems of corruption.

PHOTOCOPIABLE RESOURCES (PAGES 118–120)

3.1 can be used any time after Unit 10
3.2 can be used any time after Unit 12
3.3 can be used after Unit 12.

BUSINESS AND CULTURAL NOTES

In this module, students are confronted with a variety of issues that often come to the surface during cross-cultural interaction. Such issues include attitudes towards the authorities and the law, corruption, loyalty, and adherence to deadlines and schedules. The module focuses on these cultural factors and the related challenges for people doing business in China, Russia, Brazil and Africa. In interviews and short case studies, individuals from those cultures and foreign business people share their experiences and explain various concepts and cultural norms. Students discuss their reactions to certain attitudes and forms of behaviour, and explore them further through role plays and presentations. They also prepare advice for foreign business people and investors wishing to do business in their country.

9 A thriving economy

Reading and vocabulary
In this section students learn vocabulary such as *thriving* and *flourish* to describe emerging private sector markets.

Listening and speaking
In a listening exercise in which an economist talks about the Chinese private sector, students are presented with language to talk about the future of this growing economy.

Grammar
cause and effect
Students practise using appropriate conjunctions and linkers, such as *due to* and *as a result*, to express cause and effect in this section.

Communication
leading meetings
Students develop skills for leading meetings, managing *preparation, purpose, process* and *people*.

Business across Cultures
China
This section investigates some key values and assumptions in Chinese culture. Students then profile their own business culture in relation to six of the most important Chinese concepts.

Introductory activity

With Coursebooks closed, explain that the module theme is *money* and that the theme of this unit is *economies*. Ask the class to give examples of one or two types of economies and describe them briefly. Answers might include: *capitalist or free-market economy – very little government control, command economy – old communist USSR – government decides how to distribute goods and services, emerging and developing economies such as India and China – cost and standard of living is rising fast.* Start a unit word field around the word *economies* and add all relevant vocabulary to it.

Start-up

A Read through the questions with the class. Check comprehension if necessary. Ask pairs to discuss the questions and report their answers back to the class briefly.
Answers might include: *growing rapidly (changing all the time), the state is gradually pulling out of the more highly competitive markets* (might have completely done so by the time you read this – given the pace of change – the reading article gives a figure of 70 per cent), *the East (Beijing, Shanghai). It appears to be embracing it.*

Reading and vocabulary

A Ask the class to read the article and find answers to the questions in the start-up discussion individually. Do a class answer check.

KEY

The private sector now accounts for 70 per cent of China's GDP and employs 75 per cent of the workforce.

Private companies have flourished in two regions in particular – around Shenzhen in the south and in Zhejiang province, south-west of Shanghai, of which Hangzhou is the capital.

Under President Hu Jintao, the emphasis has been on reducing social inequality – fresh political pressure on the private sector. The other uncertainty concerns access to finance. ..., most private companies were founded using funds from friends and family or underground banks, rather than the official banks ... There are signs this is changing. Industrial and Commercial Bank of China says that it is focusing an increasing amount of its lending on small and medium-sized enterprises, which are mostly privately owned. Similarly, China Development Bank is setting up a new facility for SMEs.

B Read the questions with the class. Ask the class to do the exercise as instructed in the Coursebook individually. Do a class answer check.

KEY

1 Hangzhou is the capital of Zhejiang province, south-west of Shanghai. It is famous for its lake and its tea, and its sense of refinement.

2 Shenzhen is in the south of China, in Guangdong province close to Hong Kong. It owes its economic success to the proximity of Hong Kong and to the heavy investment by Hong Kong and Taiwanese entrepreneurs in the region.

3 Because it was neglected by Beijing.

4 1988.

5 Private entrepreneurs now face few restrictions if they start a new company, unless it is in one of the heavily regulated sectors such as telecoms, finance or media.

6 The political climate and access to finance.

7 From friends and family or underground banks.

C Get pairs to match the words and phrases in *italics* in the article with their definitions. Do a class answer check.

KEY

1 *to pin down*

2 *flourished*

3 *thriving*

4 *founded*

5 *hanging over*

6 *port of call*

7 *corridors of power*

8 *spectacular*

D Ask the class to do the exercise as instructed in the Coursebook. Do a quick class answer check.

KEY

1 *founded*

2 *port of call*

3 *flourished*

4 *spectacular*

5 *corridors of power*

6 *pin down*

7 *hanging over*

8 *thriving*

Extension activity: Ask small groups to re-read the article and brainstorm phrases for one of the following categories: phrases to describe growth, such as: *thriving, to flourish, prosper*; reasons for growth: *neglected by state-owned companies, heavy investment*; threats to growth: *legal uncertainties, big issues hanging over them*. Start up a unit word field based on the article around the phrase, *growing and developing economies*, with the three categories leading off it. Get each group to present and explain their list to the rest of the class and write up all vocabulary.

E Ask pairs to discuss how the development of the private sector in China compares with their country or another country they know well. Get them to briefly summarise their discussions to the class. If you have a multinational class, allow time to ask further questions. In monocultural classes, allow students time to comment and give their opinions. Add any useful language items which come up, to the unit word field, under appropriate categories.

Extension activity: Depending on your class, ask students to write a short article, using vocabulary items from their word field, about recent economic changes in their own country or another country they know.

▶ VOCABULARY REVIEW AND DEVELOPMENT, PAGE 90 OF THE COURSEBOOK, CAN BE DONE AT THIS STAGE.

▶ FOR FURTHER READING AND VOCABULARY PRACTICE RELATING TO THE TOPIC OF ECONOMIES, DIRECT STUDENTS TO PAGE 44 OF THE WORKBOOK.

Listening and speaking

A AUDIO **9.1** Tell students they are going to listen to an economist talking about the growth of the Chinese economy and decide whether the statements are true, false, or not given. Play the audio and do a quick class check. Ask students to give reasons for their answers.

KEY

1 NG. It exports just under $1,000 billion of manufactured goods. Nothing is mentioned about imports of raw materials.

2 F It is still just behind Germany, but will soon overtake it.

3 T

4 T

5 T

6 NG. Nothing is mentioned about exactly how big Lenovo is.

7 F It can only come from an expansion of a locally based private sector.

8 NG There should be a rise of genuinely global companies, but for the moment they are still state-owned.

AUDIO SCRIPT

Interviewer: Do you think China's going to continue growing the way it has been doing?

Economist: It's very tempting to think it will. China currently exports nearly $1,000 billion a year of manufactured goods, and is about to overtake Germany to become the world's third largest economy. And foreign investment is literally pouring into the country. But there could be trouble ahead, but it's more because of politics than economics.

Interviewer: What do you mean exactly? Can you give me some examples?

Economist: Well, take the private sector. From the outside people imagine there's a booming capitalist sector, thriving under the guidance of the government. But the reality's quite different. Private companies are still expected to work closely with provincial governments and state-owned enterprises. Basically, the government still hasn't decided if it's in favour of a truly free market, so private entrepreneurs are never sure where they stand. But things are changing all the time. For now multinationals remain very attractive to the Chinese for a variety of reasons: including the fact that they are mostly foreign and therefore do not pose a threat to the political status quo.

Interviewer: So how is all this likely to affect the economy?

Economist: Well, continued high growth can only come from an expansion of a locally-based private sector. This should eventually lead to the rise of large Chinese companies which are genuinely global. A good example of this is Lenovo, which bought IBM's PC business. This may be a sign of things to come but for now all the other big Chinese companies are still state-owned.

Extension activity: Do a second listening and ask students to pick out any interesting / difficult phrases, such as *pouring into (the country), booming, never sure where they stand*. Write them up on the board and elicit synonyms for difficult phrases. Add relevant items to the unit word field.

B Read the questions with the class, and check students' understanding of words such as *bubble* and *burst*. Ask the class to work in small groups, using the information from the audio script and their own general knowledge about China to discuss the questions. Students should spend about 20 minutes preparing notes on their answers to each of the three questions. One member of the group should control timing and put each question to the rest of the group, who should discuss it for a maximum of 10 minutes. Ask one member of the class to note down the main ideas expressed by the group and present them briefly to the class. Allow time for discussion and add useful items to the unit word field.

Grammar
Cause and effect

A Read the cause and effect rules and model sentences with the class and ask them to do the exercise as instructed in the Coursebook individually. Do a quick class check of answers.

KEY

Cause	Effect
because due to because of owing to as a result of since on account of	therefore so consequently as a result lead to cause result in

B Ask students to complete the sentences using the words and phrases in the table. Remind them that there is more than one possibility. Do a quick answer check, including students' different versions of the same sentence.

KEY

1 Due to / Because of / Owing to / As a result of / On account of

2 therefore / consequently / as a result

3 Because / Since

4 lead to / cause / result in

C Ask students to complete the sentences using the phrases *reason for* and *result of*. Do a quick class check.

KEY

1 result of   2 reason for   3 result of

Extension activity: Ask pairs to rewrite the sentences in B using a different linker from the key phrases in A and C. They should reorder the sentence structure and position of the linker, if necessary. Some possible sentences are:

The liberalisation of the Chinese economy continues, so there is more room for private enterprises to develop.

Since foreign companies are seen as less of a threat, China has gone out of its way to attract multinationals.

▶ FOR FURTHER INFORMATION ON CAUSE AND EFFECT, REFER STUDENTS TO GRAMMAR OVERVIEW, PAGE 161 OF THE COURSEBOOK.

▶ FOR SELF-STUDY EXERCISES ON CAUSE AND EFFECT, SEE PAGE 46 OF THE WORKBOOK.

▶ GRAMMAR REVIEW AND DEVELOPMENT, PAGE 90 OF THE COURSEBOOK, CAN BE DONE AT THIS STAGE.

Speaking

A Divide the class into two groups. Get each group to read through the information and check understanding together. Do a quick review of any difficult language items separately with each group. Get students to do the exercise as instructed in the Coursebook. Circulate, noting down problematic vocabulary and pronunciation problems for a class review. Before doing the review, get one or two pairs to redo the exercise in front of the class.

Communication
Leading meetings

Explain that the subject of the unit section is leading meetings. With Coursebooks closed, ask small groups to brainstorm a list of ways in which a meeting leader can ensure that the meeting is run effectively. Do a class review of answers and write them up on the board.

Possible responses:

Leading a meeting effectively

Before the meeting

Circulate information to all participants. Include the following:

   Time /Date / Location

   Background information

   Objectives

   Agenda

   Assigned items for preparation

Opening the meeting

Welcome new participants

State the objectives of the meeting

Set the agenda

Set rules of behaviour and process (For example, participants should speak clearly for the benefit of participants whose level of English is weaker)

Appoint a minutes-taker

Set the timing of the meeting

During the meeting

Introduce agenda items

Control the timing

Manage turn-taking and participant engagement

Ensure that all discussion is relevant to the agenda

Summarise each agenda item

Also:

Be as neutral as possible.

Closing the meeting

Indicate closing of the meeting

Summarise points and outcomes

Assign action items

Thank participants

Instruct the class to open their Coursebooks at page 67. Read the opening statement with the class. Refer the class back to their ideas on the board and get students to assign these to the appropriate category presented in the instruction. Do a class answer check.

A AUDIO 9.2 Read through the questions with the class. Ask students to listen to the audio and do the exercise as instructed in the Coursebook. Do a class answer check. Use the audio script to check your answers.

B Ask pairs to read phrases in the Key language box to each other. Alternatively, write out the language items on several sets of cards, and their functions on cards of a different colour and get small groups to match them up, before they read them out to the class as a review. Get the class to listen to the audio again and identify the language used to manage the meeting successfully. Do a review of any difficult items such as: *bring this together*. Elicit alternative expressions and get students to add them to the list.

KEY

Use the audio script to check your answers.

AUDIO SCRIPT

A: *OK, look let's start. I think you've all seen the memo which I sent round yesterday, so you'll know why we're having this meeting. Basically, one of our employees has gone to the press and accused us of discrimination. Now, this sort of thing can soon get out of hand so I've called this meeting to talk through the issue and to decide on how we're going to respond. Is everybody clear about that? Now, I know you all have a busy day ahead of you so I'd like to structure this carefully. We'll start by hearing from Helen. She's going to tell us what the employee is complaining about. Then I'd like to consider our options – in other words, decide on our response – and then finally we should be able to agree an action plan. Right, let's start with you Helen.*

B: *Thanks. Well, we've been contacted by the Daily Herald, asking us to confirm or deny the story told to them by Josh Reynolds. He's a packer on the finished product line and is accusing us of discrimination against men. He's saying that he and some of his colleagues are going to lose their jobs in the current round of restructuring because they're men. In other words, we favour our female employees.*

A: *OK, so I think we all understand the picture. Let's now talk about the options. Helen, what's your feeling?*

B: *Well, we've already denied this story, but of course that won't stop the press from publishing it. I think we need to put out a press release which stresses our equal opportunities policy ...*

A: *Let's try to bring this together then. So, we're going to take the following actions. Firstly, Helen is going to issue a press release which stresses our equal opportunities policy. Secondly, Peter is going to call a factory meeting in which we communicate to all the staff our trust in them and the quality of their work and finally, Max is going to contact our lawyers to make sure we're ready to fight any case for wrongful dismissal. OK. Let's stop there and we'll monitor developments and report back at our weekly meeting next Monday.*

C Quickly elicit the four Ps. Appoint a student to read through the two issues aloud. Put students into small groups and get them to do the exercise as instructed in the Coursebook. A different person should lead each item. Appoint an observer to each group to monitor observance of the four Ps and record key language items used. Ask each monitor to report their observations and language

examples of how the four Ps were managed back to the class. The Leading Meetings Feedback framework on page 124 can be used.

▶ FOR DEVELOPMENT AND CONSOLIDATION OF THE LANGUAGE ABOVE, SEE PAGE 47 OF THE WORKBOOK.

▶ REFER STUDENTS TO PAGE 149 OF THE COURSEBOOK FOR A SUMMARY OF THE POINTS COVERED IN THIS COMMUNICATION SECTION.

Business across Cultures
China

For information on China and its culture, visit the following website:
www.executiveplanet.com/index.php?title=China

Read the introduction then ask students if they can guess what challenges foreigners experience when doing business in China.

Possible responses:

Addressing others appropriately (Chinese names appear in a different order from Western names)

Gift-giving conventions (government policy forbids giving gifts in the business environment as it is considered a bribe)

Different concepts of time (the Chinese are extremely punctual)

Different working practices (the Chinese do not like to deal with people they don't know or trust)

Regard for status and hierarchy

The concept of 'saving face'

A AUDIO 9.3 Read the instructions and questions together. Play the audio once and let students compare their answers with a partner before checking them in class. Tell students that you will play the audio again and that they should listen out for more information about each of the three factors mentioned. Play the audio again and ask students to check their answers in pairs. Do a quick answer check.

KEY

1 He mentions relationships, loyalty and understanding.

2 For the sake of being agreeable.

AUDIO SCRIPT

A: *Tom, you've been doing business with China since the 70s. What sort of problems do you come across?*

B: *At the root of most problems is miscommunication. Often suppliers will agree to terms, for the sake of being agreeable – you know, they like to say 'yes'. Every detail needs to be clarified. Another problem is not knowing the right people – in China it's really important to build good relationships.*

A: *So you feel the success of the business can be directly linked to the quality of continued relationships with Chinese vendors?*

B: *That's right. The vendors in China have a tremendous amount of loyalty to the people they work with. There may be horror stories about the Chinese leaving Westerners high and dry, but if we keep our word, they keep theirs. A lot of Westerners go into Asia and expect Asia to act like the West. At the end of the day, if you act like this you won't succeed. Eat the food, enjoy the people, read the books – you have to get to know the culture.*

B If you have a multicultural class, ask people of different nationalities to work together to compare their reactions. Discuss their ideas in class. To extend this exercise, ask them what they think the Chinese would say in each of the situations.

Extension activity: Get students to role play the scenarios from different points of view: someone from their own culture, a Chinese business person and, if you have a multicultural group, a person from one of their colleagues' cultures.

C Ask students to do the exercise as indicated in the Coursebook. When going through the answers, make sure that they explain their choices.

KEY					
1f	2b	3c	4e	5d	6a

D Ask students to do the exercise in pairs. Afterwards, ask each pair to briefly summarise their discussion.

E If you have a multicultural class, ask people of different nationalities to work together and compare their business cultures in terms of the six concepts. You could ask them to create a five-minute presentation on their business cultures and to represent their values visually. Demonstrate how by describing your own cultural values aided by a chart like the one below.

Note: the values here are ranked from 1 (least valued) to 7 (most valued).

The importance of six values in my culture

Give each pair flipchart paper for their charts. In the case of pairs consisting of different nationalities, ask them to place their values side-by-side on the same chart. Ask students to include an overview of the challenges they would face in China within their presentation. Invite comments and questions from other students during the presentations.

▶ FOR SELF-STUDY WORK ON INTERCULTURAL ISSUES IN CHINA SEE PAGE 48 OF THE WORKBOOK.

▶ REFER STUDENTS TO PAGE 152 OF THE COURSEBOOK FOR A SUMMARY OF THE POINTS COVERED IN THIS BUSINESS ACROSS CULTURES SECTION.

Checklist

Review the end of unit checklist items in the Coursebook with your students, as well as the unit word field. Add any interesting pronunciation items to the pronunciation file started in Unit 1.

Final activity: Consonant_vowel linking

Write up on the board the extract, *I think you've all seen the memo which I sent round yesterday, so you'll know why we're having this meeting* from audio 9.2 on page 121.

Get pairs to read this sentence as quickly as they can! Elicit that when spoken at speed, many words appear to run into each other. There is often no audible gap between two words when the first one ends in a consonant sound and the second one begins with a vowel sound, or vice versa. This includes the sound generally produced when the word begins with a 'y'. The sound is represented by a /j/ on the phonemic chart. This is a natural effect and is known as consonant vowel linking. Get students to write an underscore _ between the words on the board which link in this way.

Model : I_think_you've_all seen the_memo_which_I_sent round_yesterday, so you'll know why we're having this meeting.

Students should underscore most of these links. Obviously, where there is a natural pause in the sentence, this phenomenon won't occur. Get pairs to practise this sentence at speed a few more times.

NB Students who have been taught to speak slowly and enunciate every word clearly, can find this quite unnatural, often believing they must be incomprehensible to others, when in fact to a *native speaker,* they sound more natural. Students shouldn't be required to reproduce this natural fast speech phenomenon if they are uncomfortable with it, or you feel it isn't necessary, but awareness of the linking effect of fast speech could help them to decode natural speed native speaker speech more easily.

Ask pairs to go through the first paragraph of audio script on page 121, reading it out quickly to each other and marking in where they expect to hear a consonant _vowel or vowel_consonant link. Then listen to the audio to check their answers.

Divide the remaining parts of audio 9.2 between pairs, ask them to repeat the exercise, and get them to read out their paragraphs to the class, as a final review.

Model answer

Where the speakers decide to pause for breath, or emphasise a word, they will not actually occur in the audio. Links produced when an intrusive /w/ sound is produced between *so /w/ I've,* for example are not included. Students may notice them however. You can mention that this effect does indeed produce a consonant_vowel sound link and will be tackled in the final activity in unit 10. Although intrusive /r/ is only introduced in the unit 12 final activity, its resulting linking effect is included in this answer because, as the letter is actually written down, it is possibly more obvious to students.

A: OK, look, let's start. I think_you've_all seen the_memo_which_I_sent round yesterday, so you'll know why we're having this meeting. Basically, one_of_our_employees has gone to_the_press_and_accused_us_of discrimination. Now, this sort_of thing can soon get_out_of hand so I've called this meeting to talk through the issue and to_decide_on how we're going to_respond. Is_ everybody_clear_about that? Now, I_know you_all have_a_busy_day ahead_of_you so I'd like to structure this carefully. We'll start by hearing from Helen. She's going to_ tell_us what the employee is complaining_about. Then_I'd like to_consider_our_options – in_other words, decide on_our response - and then finally we_should be able to agree an_action plan. Right, let's start with you, Helen.

B: Thanks. Well, we've been contacted by_ the_*Daily_Herald*,
asking_us to confirm_or deny_the_story_told to_them
by_Josh Reynolds. He's_a_packer_on the_finished product
line_and_is_accusing_us_of discrimination_against men.
He's saying that he and some_of his colleagues_are going
to_lose their jobs_in the_current round_of restructuring
because they're men. In_other words, we_favour_our
female_employees.

A: OK, so I_think we all_understand the_picture. Let's now
talk_about the options. Helen, what's_your feeling?

B: Well, we've_already denied this story, but_of course that
won't stop the press from publishing_it. I_think we_need to
put_out_a_press release which
stresses_our_equal_opportunities policy.

A: Let's try to_bring this together then. So, we're going to
take the following_actions. Firstly, Helen_is going to issue
a_press release which stresses_our_equal_opportunities
policy. Secondly, Peter_is going to call_a factory meeting_in
which we_communicate to all the_staff_our trust_in
them_and the_quality of their work_and finally, Max_is
going to contact_our lawyers to_make sure we're
ready_to_fight_any case for wrongful dismissal. OK. Let's
stop there_and we'll monitor developments_and report
back_at_our weekly_meeting next Monday.

10 Foreign investment

Reading and speaking

This section deals with the vocabulary relating to foreign direct investment, such as *mergers and acquisitions, growth rate,* as well as a variety of financial figures.

Vocabulary and listening

Students tackle a range of idiomatic expressions to talk about investing in foreign markets such as, *to weigh something up, to get bogged down in.*

Grammar

referring and sequencing

Students review referring and sequencing language such as *this, that* and *these* in this section.

Communication

participating in meetings

This section gets students to practise different types of questions, useful for participating and influencing decisions in meetings.

Business cross Cultures

Russia

This section looks at Russia and its culture, particularly in relation to the investment opportunities in this part of the world.

Introductory activity

With Coursebooks closed, tell the class that the unit theme is foreign investment. Find out if there has been much historical or recent foreign investment in your students' country / countries. Ask questions such as: *Which countries have invested money in your country? Which industries have attracted foreign investment? Has the amount of foreign investment increased or decreased much in the last few years? Has your country invested in other countries? Is your country ideal for foreign investment in the future?* If so, find out what resources attract foreign investment. Answers might include: *cheaper labour, raw materials, specialist skills such as IT.* Allow students time to explain their answers. Start a unit word field around the phrase *foreign investment.*

Start-up

A Instruct the class to open their Coursebooks at page 70. Read the opening statement with the class. Elicit the meaning of difficult vocabulary such as, *studded, land mine, laced, vein, riddled.* If necessary explain the vocabulary items and draw an imaginary gold field on the board, getting students to draw in the features described. Get pairs to discuss the questions and do a class feedback. Answers might include: *mergers, takeovers, building new production facilities.*

Reading and speaking

A Ask students to read the article about foreign direct investment.

B Read through the questions with the class. Check comprehension of BRIC (Brazil, Russia, India and China). Do a class answer check. Elicit that a *trillion* equals one million million in the US and is generally accepted worldwide.

KEY

1 *The total amount of FDI worldwide in 2006.*

2 *New investment to expand a company's activities in that country.*

3 *The US.*

4 *A result of mergers and acquisitions.*

5 *$70m.*

6 *Brazil, Russia, India and China.*

C Ask pairs to practise saying the figures aloud and go round the class eliciting the correct pronunciation of these number phrases. Write *per cent* on the board. Elicit that the word stress falls on *cent,* and the *per* is quite short, in contrast to the *per* in *person.* $1.23 trillion, should be pronounced *one point two three* (not twenty three). Elicit that although the $ sign is written before the number, it is spoken after the number. Ask a student to write $177.3m out in words on the board. Make sure that the *and* is not forgotten between the *one hundred* and the *seventy.*

D Ask a student to read the article to the class. Find out any UK companies which students know have been taken over by foreign companies Examples: *BAA's (British Airport Authority) takeover by the Spanish company Ferrovial, Orange (mobile network operator) by France Telecom* and if they know of any changes to these companies resulting from their takeover. Encourage students to explain as much as possible. Elicit any upsides or downsides which have resulted for either the UK workforce, public, or the foreign parent company. If you think your class might have difficulty brainstorming this subject, if necessary give out a few short case study articles from the national press or the Internet as preparation homework. Ask students to work in two groups to brainstorm the question items. Get the two groups to hold their debate. As they debate, write up useful phrases relating to foreign investment on the unit word field.

E Put students into pairs and get them to make a list. Encourage them to think of both positive and negative changes. Answers might include: *restructuring, asset stripping and selling off parts of the company, redundancies, added investment, improved profitability.* Do a class review and allow time for students to ask questions and debate. Write up any useful vocabulary on the board.

▶ FOR FURTHER READING AND VOCABULARY PRACTICE RELATING TO THE TOPIC OF FOREIGN INVESTMENT, DIRECT STUDENTS TO PAGE 49 OF THE WORKBOOK.

Vocabulary and listening

A Ask pairs to brainstorm all the factors which need to be taken into account when investing in a foreign country. If necessary, write up the categories, *infrastructure, workforce, materials, taxation, law, cultural knowledge, language,* and ask the class to consider those areas as well as any others they can think of. Do a class review of answers. Add their ideas to the unit word field.

B Ask the class to match the phrases *in italics* with their definitions. Do a class check.

KEY

1e	2d	3j	4c	5f	6a	7b	8h	9i	10g

C AUDIO **10.1** Tell the class to listen to an interview with Richard Parker, a specialist in country risk analysis and note down the factors he says you should take into account when investing abroad. Play the audio. Do a class comprehension check of answers and ask the class to compare them with their brainstormed lists from A. Add any new phrases to the unit word field.

KEY

the state of the local economy – GDP, inflation rates, labour costs and the size of the domestic and neighbouring markets.

skill levels of the labour force

the industrial relations climate

financial and regulatory aspects – the stability of the currency, exchange control regulations if any

whether there're any government incentives on offer for inward investment

political stability

security and safety

government attitude to foreign investment – do they encourage or discourage it? Do they insist on a local partner? Can you remit profits out of the country?

D Ask the class to listen again to find out which country is mentioned as being high-risk and why. Do a class answer check. Add any new phrases to the unit word field.

KEY

Russia is mentioned as a high-risk country. He does recommend investing in Russia because the potential market is huge and it has a lot to offer. However, they need to weigh up all the risks and invest in the long term.

AUDIO SCRIPT

Interviewer:	What are the main things a company should be concerned about when planning an investment in a foreign country?
Richard Parker:	Well, you need to look at things from two angles. First, what are the positive points, which may encourage a company to invest in a country? This would include things such as the state of the local economy – GDP, inflation rates, labour costs and the size of the domestic and neighbouring markets. You also need to take into account the skill levels of the labour force and the industrial relations climate – is there a history of industrial unrest and strikes, for example? Finally, there are financial and regulatory aspects – the stability of the currency, exchange control regulations if any, and whether there're any government incentives on offer for inward investment.
Interviewer:	And what about the negative things – the so-called risk factors? Where do they come into the equation?
Richard Parker:	The first thing to consider is political stability. This doesn't mean that the country has to be a fully fledged democracy, only that it's relatively stable and not likely to descend into chaos. Related to that is the issue of security and safety. Then there's the government attitude to foreign investment. Do they encourage or discourage it? Do they insist on a local partner? Can you remit profits out of the country?
Interviewer:	And are there certain parts of the world which are high risk for investment?
Richard Parker:	The risks of investment in certain parts of Africa are well known, but closer to home I'd say to invest in Russia can also be risky. There's still some corruption and money laundering going on and central government and local legislation keep changing. One particular sector where companies have had their fingers burnt is the oil and gas industry. Russia has huge reserves and in the confusion of the 1990s the foreign oil giants were able to move in and take controlling interests in some of the large exploration projects. But the political climate has changed, and the government now wants to have control of its natural resources so it can get the full benefit from them, especially with the oil price being so high.
Interviewer:	So would you recommend companies invest in Russia?
Richard Parker:	So long as they weigh up all the risks and go in for the long term, I would say yes, depending on the product or service they're offering. The potential market is huge and it has a lot of offer. But you have to be able to live with the risk of things not working out quite as planned, and you really need some local help.

E Look at the model noun group with the class and ask students to form other noun groups with the words in the exercise. Do a quick class answer check.

KEY

1g   2i   3d   4j   5c   6h   7k   8e   9f   10b   11a

F Ask pairs to repeat the noun groups in E to each other, making sure they put the main stress on the correct word or syllable in each case. Then play the interview again to check pronunciation and do a final round the class pronunciation check. Write any difficult words on the board and mark in the correct stress pattern.

▶ VOCABULARY REVIEW AND DEVELOPMENT, PAGE 91 OF THE COURSEBOOK, CAN BE DONE AT THIS STAGE.

Grammar

Referring and sequencing

A Read the *referring* rules and model sentences with the class. Ask them to look at the sentences from the interview and do the exercise individually. Do a quick class answer check.

KEY

1 This factor ...

2 These ...

3 This problem ...

B Read the instructions with the class. Ask the class to re-read the audio script on page 122 and answer the questions individually. Do a class answer check.

KEY

1 The two angles are the positive and negative aspects of investing in a country. The first is introduced by First, and the second by the interviewer, who says: And **what about** the negative thing ...

2 Positive angle: things such as ..., also, Finally

Negative angle: The first thing ..., Related to that ..., Then

Extension activity: Ask students to use the model linkers and sentences to write a short paragraph on the positive and negative aspects of investing in their own country. Get each student to read their paragraph out to the class in a review.

▶ FOR FURTHER INFORMATION ON REFERRING AND SEQUENCING, REFER STUDENTS TO GRAMMAR OVERVIEW, PAGE 162 OF THE COURSEBOOK.

▶ FOR SELF-STUDY EXERCISES ON REFERRING AND SEQUENCING, SEE PAGE 51 OF THE WORKBOOK.

▶ GRAMMAR REVIEW AND DEVELOPMENT, PAGE 91 OF THE COURSEBOOK, CAN BE DONE AT THIS STAGE.

▶ PHOTOCOPIABLE 3.1, PAGE 118, CAN NOW BE DONE.

Information exchange

A Read the instruction with the class and get them to do the exercise as indicated in the Coursebook. Encourage them to check and clarify figures and spell out words their partner isn't familiar with. Do a class check on the information, reviewing pronunciation of numbers and difficult vocabulary items, which might include, *stable, fragmented, urbanisation, aspirations.*

B Divide the class into groups with a balance of A and B students. Get each group to appoint a leader and a different person to note down the main points of the meeting. Ask each group to hold a meeting to decide which country to invest in. Get the group reporter to report the main arguments and resulting decisions back to the class after the exercise. Add useful phrases to the unit word field.

Communication

Participating in meetings

With Coursebooks closed, ask students to form small groups and brainstorm a set of rules for meeting participants which will help to ensure that the meeting is effective.

Compare and discuss responses in class.

Possible responses:

Do:

Arrive on time

Be well-prepared

Support the chair in moving the agenda ahead

Contribute to discussions

Encourage others to give their views

Actively listen to others and ask questions

Be concise and to the point

Speak clearly for participants who have a lower level of English

Check and clarify information if you do not understand

Be constructive / Avoid critical or conflictive language

Do not:

Dominate the discussion

Constantly interrupt other participants

Take rejection of your ideas personally

Deviate from the agenda

A Read the opening statement with the class. Ask them to look at the Key language box and do the exercise as instructed in the Coursebook. Do a quick class answer check.

KEY

1b   2c   3d   4f   5a   6e

B AUDIO **10.2** Tell the class to listen to six extracts from a meeting and identify the question type they hear from the Key language box. Play the audio more than once if necessary and get students to compare their answers with a partner. Do a quick class check.

KEY

1f   2d   3a   4b   5e   6c

AUDIO SCRIPT

1

A: I will be visiting St Petersburg next week actually.

B: That's good. Can we make sure we all know what the next steps are?

2

A: Really, there are lots of opportunities.

B: I see that, but don't you think that's a difficult market to break into?

A: No, no more than anywhere else. Of course it's different and we need to adapt our products and especially our distribution.

3

A: So, I have drawn up a shortlist of agents we could use.

B: What exactly do you mean by agents? I mean, are they going to be our distributors?

A: Well, yes. In some cases they could do this as well ...

4

A: Well I've been working incredibly hard to find these people and you've got to remember that it's a massive country.

B: So, you're really feeling pretty stretched?

A: You can say that again. I haven't been home for a full weekend in months.

5

A: Let's see where we've got to. We have agreed to go ahead with the Moscow company. Is that right?

B: Absolutely. I have already talked to ...

6

A: I have been spending a lot of time in Russia recently and I think there's lots of potential.

B: Could you elaborate on that a little? You know, what have you seen that brings you to this conclusion?

A: Well mainly that consumers are now looking to upgrade ...

C Get students to work in pairs and do the exercise as indicated in the Coursebook. First, read the instruction and project choices with the class and check vocabulary. Ask each pair to decide on an investment project and then hold a short meeting with their partner. Ask students to tick off each type of question from the Key language box when their partner asks it. The Participating in Meetings Feedback framework on page 125 can be used.

▶ FOR DEVELOPMENT AND CONSOLIDATION OF THE LANGUAGE ABOVE, SEE PAGE 52 OF THE WORKBOOK.

▶ REFER STUDENTS TO PAGE 149 OF THE COURSEBOOK FOR A SUMMARY OF THE POINTS COVERED IN THIS COMMUNICATION SECTION.

Business across Cultures

Russia

A comprehensive overview of Russia and its culture can be found on the following website:
www.executiveplanet.com/index.php?title=Russia

With Coursebooks closed, ask students what an investor should consider before investing in a foreign country. Do this as a whole class exercise and write their ideas on the board.

Possible responses:

The economy

Laws and policies

Tax rates

Infrastructure

Competition

Availability of domestic raw materials and natural resources

Extent of the target market

Political climate

Law and order / Stability

Geography / Climate / Location

Cultural values and attitudes

Instruct students to open their books and then read the introduction together.

A Read the article together by asking two students to read it out loud in class. Afterwards, deal with any vocabulary queries by getting students to provide definitions for each other. Ask students to write a checklist in pairs and draw their attention to the beginning of the checklist (Advantages and Disadvantages) that they must complete. Compare answers in class.

KEY

Advantages	**Disadvantages**
rich natural resources	high unemployment
annual growth	high inflation
100 per cent literacy	lack of industrial equipment
infrastructure	law and order
proximity to Europe	government influence
nuclear power	

B Before embarking on this exercise, ask students to work in small groups and brainstorm their perceptions of the Russians. Allow them up to 5 minutes to note their ideas on flipchart paper then ask them to share their ideas with the rest of the class. Do they share a similar perception of the Russians?

Some typical perceptions:

We perceive the Russians as

hospitable

emotional

bureaucratic

suspicious

strong

serious

intellectual

Finally, reveal how the Russians perceive themselves.

The Russians perceive themselves as

loyal

well-educated

hierarchical

undisciplined

broad-minded

relationship-oriented

passive

emotional

creative / artistic

Were any of the students' perceptions right?

Next, draw students' attention to exercise B. Check understanding of 'cultural fit'. This came up in Unit 1 and refers to the way in which a merging partner company or individual shares your cultural values, expectations and attitudes. When students are exchanging information ask them to close their books so that they don't simply read the texts to each other. Get students to discuss the question with their partner then share their thoughts with the rest of the class.

C In a monocultural group, ask students to do the exercise as indicated in the Coursebook. Set a time limit of 20 minutes to prepare the checklist then get them to present their checklists within small groups. Each presentation should take no longer than 5 minutes.

In the case of a multicultural group, you could ask students to imagine that they are trying to convince foreign investors (students of other nationalities) to invest in their own countries. Encourage the 'investors' to ask questions and, in the end, decide which country they would prefer to invest in and explain why.

Extension activity:
Culture-specific words

Explain that Russian words and vocabulary reveal a lot about Russian cultural values. Give the following examples (and write the words in **bold** on the board as you go along):

■ *In Russia, there is an abundance of 'active emotional verbs', both positive and negative, which are very 'physical' whereas in English emotions are treated as passive states that are caused by external forces.*

■ *'Diminutive forms' (e.g. Andy for Andrew in English) exist for almost every name in Russian. These are used with both children and adults without distinction of age or gender and in a range of contexts.*

■ *There is also the use of 'culture-specific words', which are not really translatable in any other language, like dusha – a term which expresses 'soul, emotion and thought'. It has been used frequently in Russian literature to describe Russian spirituality and Russians are fond of using this word in most situations.*

Ask students what this tells us about Russian culture.

Possible responses:

Active emotional verbs → Russians are open about their feelings and emotions.

Diminutive forms → They are comfortable expressing closeness, affection and intimacy in a range of contexts.

Culture-specific words –'Dusha' → Russians tend to describe life and events from a religious or spiritual perspective. In Russia, the soul is the key to a person's identity and behaviour.

Tell students that every society has its own social norms which are often reflected in the language. Write 'whinge' on the board then explain the following:

The verb 'to whinge' is culture-specific to Australia. It means to complain a lot in an annoying manner about something which does not seem important. The use of this word dates back to the time when the first settlers in Australia were very dependent on each other. During these extremely hard and dangerous times, whinging and expressing pessimism was seen as bad manners and a lack of consideration for other people's feelings.

Ask students what this culture-specific word tells us about modern Australians. Allow them to discuss this in pairs for 2 minutes then get them to share their ideas in class. Write their responses on the board.

Possible responses and additional information:

Australians do not respect people who complain about unimportant issues.

Australians are likely to be more 'stoical' when irritated by something.

They are more optimistic and positive – If you ask an Australian how things are going, the response will be 'Good, thanks'. And, when confronted with a 'whinger' (a person who complains), they tend to give advice such as 'take it easy' and 'it will be all right'.

Finally, ask students if they can think of any culture-specific words in their own language with roots in culture, history, literature or even folk tales. What do these words tell us about their culture? If possible, divide the class into small groups of the same nationality to discuss these questions for 10 minutes. If you have a very culturally diverse class, get students to work in groups of four and compare their culture-specific words; in this case, to give everyone the chance to describe and compare their words, allow up to 20 minutes. If students have difficulty thinking of words, help them by asking them to consider the following:

Think about how you describe the weather / family members / time / being late / feelings and emotions / behaviour/ food / tastes / animals / etc.?

Afterwards, get each group to present the words that they identified and explain what they tell us about their culture. Encourage the other students to make comments and ask questions. In a multicultural class, invite students to compare the words being presented with words in other languages. What do the differences or similarities between the ways they describe or express things show?

▶ FOR A READING ACTIVITY ON RUSSIA SEE PAGE 53 OF THE WORKBOOK.

▶ REFER STUDENTS TO PAGE 153 OF THE COURSEBOOK FOR A SUMMARY OF THE POINTS COVERED IN THIS BUSINESS ACROSS CULTURES SECTION.

Checklist

Review the end of unit checklist items in the Coursebook with your students, as well as the unit word field. Add any interesting pronunciation items to the pronunciation file started in Unit 1.

Final activity: Noun_noun linking: intrusive /w/

Write these phrases from audio 10.1 on the board. Ask students to practise saying them quickly. Alternatively, say the phrases very quickly (or audio record yourself saying them a few times) and ask students to write down what they hear.

Elicit that between the vowel sounds at the end of the one word and the beginning of the next, an extra (intrusive) /w/ sound can be heard. This is one of the reasons why students can sometimes fail to correctly recognise a phrase such as *two angles*, hearing *two_wangles* instead, or *go_win* instead of *go in*. This can be particularly confusing when the word students think they hear (such as *win*), actually exists in English.

w	w	w
two_angles	to_invest	you_also
to take into_account	the issue_of security	go_in for the long term

81

Ask pairs to choose another audio script in the Coursebook, and look for a few examples of intrusive /w/ in key business expressions to present to the class. This could be done as a homework exercise and recorded in the pronunciation file, started at the beginning of the Coursebook. If students are interested, they can repeat the exercise with intrusive /r/ and /j/.

11 The bottom line

Reading

In this section students learn a range of vocabulary such as *overheads* and *staffing levels*, to enable them to discuss how to keep a small business afloat during a recession.

Listening and speakng

Students listen to a presentation of a budget breakdown and learn terms such as *to add up to* and *to come to just over*.

Grammar

prepositions

Students learn a range of multi-word prepositions such as, *according to* (my calculations) for more sophisticated explanations.

ommunication

negotiations 1: Bargaining

Students practise bargaining, using a range of bargaining expressions such as, *provided that* and *on condition that*.

usiness across Cultures

Brazil

This section explores Brazilian values and attitudes, particularly in relation to negotiating. Students then prepare advice about negotiating in their own cultures.

Introductory activity

With Coursebooks closed, write the quotation on page 76 on the board. Ask pairs to read and discuss the quotation. Get a few students to explain how good or bad they are at sticking to a budget!

Start-up

A Instruct the class to open their Coursebooks at page 76. Elicit what the title expression refers to: *the bottom line of the profit and loss account or income statement – net profit or net income after all the expenses of operating the business have been met and corporation tax has been deducted from the gross profit figure*. It doesn't directly relate to *budgets*, although by reducing *departmental budgets*, for example, a company can save money, and as long as it continues to make the same *revenue* from its activities, can therefore increase its *gross profit*. Elicit *expenditure* as being the word for *the amount a business spends in the course of business* and *revenue*, as being the *money earned from business dealings*. Elicit that budgets are only a *projected figure, an estimation of what you will spend*. If people *overspend* then the budget becomes *overrun*.

B Find out whether students have to manage a budget. This could apply to higher education students as well as company employees or self-employed people. Elicit examples of both good and bad budgeting and what makes budgets overrun. Answers might include: *unforeseen expenses, lack of discipline, prices rising, poor information before the project*. Start up a unit word field around the word *budgeting*. Ask pairs to discuss the question and do a class review. Write up all useful language around the word field.

Reading

A Read the first question with the class and check the meaning of *economic downturns* and *recessions*. Elicit examples of these which students have experienced in their own countries and what caused them. Answers might include: *war, political coup, rising oil prices, downturn in export partner countries, rise in exchange rate, rise in US interest rates, collapse of a number of large companies or an industry*. Then, ask them to discuss the second question with a partner and get students to report back on their discussions. Add any useful language to the word field. Answers might include: *sales figures went down, profits went down, redundancies occurred, the business went bankrupt, went out of business, went under, went bust*. Read the article title with the class. Elicit a couple of typical measures a small business can take to survive an economic recession.

B Ask students to read the article individually.

C Get students to do the exercise individually before comparing answers with a partner. Do a class check of answers and comprehension check of difficult vocabulary items.

KEY

1 *Cash flow*

2 *Investment*

3 *Inventory*

4 *Promotional expenditure*

5 *Premises*

6 *Overheads*

7 *Skills*

8 *Staffing levels*

9 *Staff input*

Extension activity: The article is rich in business word partnerships. Divide the class into three groups. Get one group to pick out expressions relating to managing a downturn, such as, *monitor financial health*, the second group to find phrases relating to saving money, such as, *delay purchase (of high cost items)* and the third group to find phrases relating to expanding the business, such as, *subletting (excess) office space*. Do a class review and add useful vocabulary items to the unit word field. Where possible, put opposites together to aid learning and memorising.

D Ask your class to work in small groups to brainstorm other recommendations. Ask one person from each group to present their list to the class. Add useful vocabulary to the unit word field. If necessary, prompt students with a few board items, such as: *Diversification, (adapt your service / extend your product range), Staffing (take on student trainees – intelligent / free / want the experience)*. Add useful vocabulary items to the unit word field.

▶ VOCABULARY REVIEW AND DEVELOPMENT, PAGE 91 OF THE COURSEBOOK, CAN BE DONE AT THIS STAGE.

Listening and speaking

A Ask pairs to do the vocabulary categorising exercise together and do a quick class check.

KEY

Equal to $	Approximately $	More than $	Less than $
To work out at $	To be in the region of $	To be just over $	To be just under $
To come to $	To be approximately $	To exceed $	To be just short of $
To cost $	To be $ at most		To be almost $
To add up to $	To be $ maximum		
To total $	To be around $		
To amount to $			
To set us back $			

B AUDIO 11.1 Tell the class they are going to listen to Tom Finchley talking about a conference budget. Get students to do the exercise as instructed in the Coursebook reminding them they should only fill in columns 1–4 at this stage. Get students to compare their answers with a partner and do a class answer check.

KEY

Two-day professional motivation conference

Budget item	Unit cost	No. units	Estimated cost	Notes
1 Conference venue (two days)	$9,000	1	**$9,000**	Charlotte Hotel. Downtown Chicago. Right atmosphere.
2 Promotion / Invitations				—
Advertising in journals	$100	8	$800	Send to the Journal of Business and Chicago Business, for example
Posters	$5	50	$250	Send to Chamber of Commerce and Chicago Business Forum
Invitations / Postage	$0.65	3,000	$1,950	Send to everyone on the mailing list. A local printer offered a special deal
Subtotal	—	—	**$3,000**	—
3 Guest speakers				Angela Perkins who spoke at the Annual Women's Leadership Exchange Simon Chapman and Lily Chang. Mario Castello whose book's being published in August
Fees	$3,000	4	$12,000	Thought Angela Perkins would ask for more
Subtotal	—	—	**$12,000**	—
4 Handouts	$2	2,000	**$4,000**	Programmes / Evaluation forms. Could get a company to donate the copying in exchange for advertising
5 Insurance	$2,000	1	**$2,000**	—
		Total	**$30,000**	—

C Ask them to listen again and make notes relating to each budget item and compare their answers with a partner. Read the example with the class first.

AUDIO SCRIPT

Hello, everybody. Well, I've worked out the budget for our conference in September.

As you can see, there are five main items on the budget.

Well, let's start with the first item: the conference venue. As you know, the conference will be for 2,000 people, so I've looked at venues of an appropriate size. The Charlotte Hotel, right in the heart of downtown Chicago, is certainly our best option. I think it's completely in line with the atmosphere we want to create. However, it doesn't come cheaply at $9,000 for two days.

Moving on! The next item is promotion and invitations. By putting advertisements in local journals and magazines, such as The Journal of Business *and* Chicago Business in Print, *we'll reach our target audience. This will cost in the region of $100 per ad and I reckon we'll need eight of them, at the most.*

With regard to nice, glossy posters, we'll need about 50, so at $5 each they'll set us back $250. We can send them to places like the Chamber of Commerce and the Chicago Business Forum.

As for invitations, we'll send them to everyone on our mailing list. That's currently 3,000. A local printer does very good ones. Unfortunately, he's not prepared to provide sponsorship, but he's offered us a special deal. Together with envelopes and postage, they will be 65 cents each. We're sending 3,000 so that'll come to $1,950.

So, the subtotal for promotions and invitations will be $3,000 at the most.

The third item: our guest speakers. What a line up this year! Angela Perkins, who spoke at the Annual Women's Leadership Exchange in Chicago last year, will be our first speaker. And, contrary to our expectations, we've managed to convince Simon Chapman and Lily Chang to speak. And thanks to Ben here and his powers of persuasion, we've got Mario Castello, which is great timing as his book's being published in August. Anyway, this is all beside the point.

Our speakers' fees will be $3,000 per person maximum. We had expected Angela Perkins to ask for more ... So that adds up to $12,000 for four speakers.

I haven't included speakers' travel expenses on account of the fact they're all Chicago based.

So, item number four: handouts. By this, I mean programmes and simple evaluation forms. We could get a local printer to donate these in exchange for advertising. By doing that, we'd save a considerable sum of money because the best quote I've had works out at about $2 per guest, which would amount to $4,000.

And, finally, item five, which is insurance. For this type of event we're looking at about $2,000.

*So, according to my calculations, that all works out at
$30,000. And, all going well, with the attendance fees we
certainly won't be running at a loss. So, let's go through that
again step by step and hear what you've got to say about it.*

D Ask pairs to spend 10 minutes brainstorming and making
notes on likely expense items of one of the topics in the
question. They should then take a little longer to prepare a
budget breakdown, using the audio script on page 123 as a
model for key language items. Give pairs a short time to
practise delivering it together. Ask each pair to make a very
short presentation of their budget breakdown on the board
to the rest of the class. Review pronunciation of numbers
as well as use of target language.

▶ FOR FURTHER READING AND VOCABULARY PRACTICE RELATING TO
THE TOPIC OF BUDGETS, DIRECT STUDENTS TO PAGE 54 OF THE
WORKBOOK.

Grammar
Prepositions

A Read the rules and examples of multi-word prepositions
with the class. Ask individuals to read the audio script on
page 123 and do the exercise as instructed in the
Coursebook. Do a class answer check.

KEY

in line with the atmosphere we want to create

As for invitations

contrary to our expectations

thanks to Ben here and his powers of persuasion

on account of the fact they're all Chicago based

According to my calculations

B Get the class to do this exercise individually and do a quick
class check.

KEY
1d
2c
3a
4e
5b

C Ask the class to do this exercise individually, then ask pairs
to compare answers. Do a class review of the alternative
answers provided in the key.

KEY

1 As for / In terms of / With regard to
2 according to / depending on
3 except for / apart from
4 In view of
5 Thanks to
6 in spite of
7 as well as / in addition to

D Get pairs to do this exercise and do a class answer check.

Model answers

by no means: *not at all, not by any means, not in any way*

at the most: *maximum, not more, tops, at the (very)*

beside the point: irrelevant, off the subject, by the way

E Get small groups to do this exercise. Instruct them to
include as many multi-word prepositions as possible.

F Get each member of the group to present part of the
group's budget. Appoint observers to note down and review
the prepositions used.

▶ FOR FURTHER INFORMATION ON PREPOSITIONS, REFER STUDENTS TO
GRAMMAR OVERVIEW, PAGE 163 OF THE COURSEBOOK.

▶ GRAMMAR REVIEW AND DEVELOPMENT, PAGE 92 OF THE
COURSEBOOK, CAN BE DONE AT THIS STAGE.

Communication
Negotiations 1: Bargaining

Ask the class if any of them have ever participated in a
negotiation before. Get one or two students to describe briefly,
what it was about, who was involved and whether it was
difficult, whether the outcome was successful etc. Alternatively,
ask the class to brainstorm a few typical negotiation contexts
such as: *negotiating a pay rise, a sale, a supply contract.*

Read the opening explanations with the class. Elicit that
conditional sentences can be useful in a bargaining situation.
Check students' understanding of the word *parties.*

A AUDIO 11.2 Tell the class to listen to the four negotiations
extracts and match the offers to the conditions using one
of the connectors in the box.

KEY

1 *a discount   provided that   place your first order today*
2 *better payment terms   so long as
   guarantee regular orders*
3 *an exclusive deal   on condition that
   promote the products nationally*
4 *a smaller order   if   order a minimum quantity*

AUDIO SCRIPT
1
*Well, it's difficult but I suppose we could offer you better
payment terms so long as you can guarantee to make orders
on a monthly basis.*
2
*Perhaps we could consider a discount, provided that you put
in an order straight away.*
3
*We'll be happy to accept a smaller order if you keep to a
minimum order quantity.*
4
*What would you think if we offered you an exclusive deal on
condition that you promise to promote our products across
your market?*

B AUDIO 11.3 Ask students to do the exercise individually and
do a class answer check.

KEY

1d   2b   3a   4c

AUDIO SCRIPT

11.3

1

A: *Well, it's difficult but I suppose we could offer you better payment terms so long as you can guarantee to make orders on a monthly basis.*

B: *I'm afraid we're not in a position to do that.*

2

A: *Perhaps we could consider a discount, provided that you put in an order straight away.*

B: *That would be difficult at the moment, but maybe next week.*

3

A: *We'll be happy to accept a smaller order if you keep to a minimum order quantity.*

B: *Yes, that sounds fine.*

4

A: *What would you think if we offered you an exclusive deal on condition that you promise to promote our products across your market?*

B: *I think we could accept that as long as you can support us with promotional material.*

B Ask the class to do the exercise in pairs, as instructed in the Coursebook. Get one or two pairs to do the role play in front of the class. Appoint observers to note down and comment on the language used. Do a final review of key language. The Negotiation Feedback framework on page 126 can be used.

▶ FOR DEVELOPMENT AND CONSOLIDATION OF THE LANGUAGE ABOVE, SEE PAGE 57 OF THE WORKBOOK.

▶ REFER STUDENTS TO PAGE 149 OF THE COURSEBOOK FOR A SUMMARY OF THE POINTS COVERED IN THIS COMMUNICATION SECTION.

Business across Cultures

Brazil

For further exploration of Brazil's culture, see the following website: www.executiveplanet.com/index.php?title=Brazil

Read the introduction together.

A Before embarking on this exercise, write the following sentence on the board:

Rules are there to be broken.

Ask students whether they agree with the sentence. Why? Why not?

In a multicultural class, ask students of different nationalities to work together and compare the role rules have on doing business in their countries. Get the pairs to summarise their findings of their discussions for the rest of the class.

B Ask different students to read each text out loud in class. Get students to provide definitions of words that others do not know. Instruct students to do the exercise in pairs then compare their answers in class.

KEY

1 It stifles economic growth.

2 Economic progress occurs when the bureaucrats sleep.

3 Business transactions are done through a despachante (middleman).

4 Some businesses keep some transactions and records off the books.

C In a multicultural class, ask students of the same nationality to work together either in groups or pairs. If this is not possible, get students of different nationalities to compare their cultures in small groups. Allow up to 5 minutes for this. Ask one person from each group to summarise their discussion and invite comments and questions from other groups. In the case of a monocultural class, do the students agree with other groups' perceptions of their own culture?

D AUDIO **11.4** Read the instructions together. Play the audio once and get students to compare their answers with a partner. Do a class answer check.

KEY

time   negotiation   breaks   titles

AUDIO SCRIPT

Interviewer:	*What should people take into account when doing business in Brazil?*
Maria Fernandes:	*A key point to consider when doing business in Brazil is that business is seen as any other sort of social interaction. For example, if you call up a business partner in Brazil, be prepared to chat first and then talk business second. Whether it is asking about their children or chatting about the latest news or soccer results, don't get straight to the point. This is something Brazilians find quite aggressive.*
Interviewer:	*I see. I've heard that coffee breaks are a way of life. Is this true?*
Maria Fernandes:	*Oh yes, expect to be interrupted! And you had better like strong, dark coffee. You won't find milky coffees in Brazil! Coffee will be offered to you when you arrive, and several times during the day.*
Interviewer:	*How do you address each other? Do you use first names?*
Maria Fernandes:	*Only use a first name if you are invited to do so. When meeting someone for the first time, address them formally. The American way of using first names in the workplace is quite disconcerting to Brazilians, who are accustomed to very defined social status and ways of addressing each other. It is a good idea to keep your distance, linguistically speaking. At least at the beginning.*
Interviewer:	*What about attitudes towards time?*

Maria Fernandes: *The perception of time and the concept of punctuality are very different in Brazil, but I insist, it has nothing to do with Brazilians being lazy. It just means that their working day doesn't follow the same rigid structure. When scheduling meetings, allow for some degree of lateness. In the US, punctuality and time-keeping are both very important. In Brazil, they are happy to do many things at the same time, so interruptions and diversions are far more common.*

E Play the audio more than once if necessary to allow students time to make notes. Ask students to compare their answers with a partner then check in class.

KEY

1 Be prepared to chat first and talk business second.

2 Only use first names if invited to do so.

3 Allow for a degree of lateness.

F Ask students to do the exercise in pairs then compare answers in class. Do a class answer check.

KEY

1c   2b   3d   4e   5a

G In the case of a monocultural class, ask students to do the exercise as indicated in small groups. Set a time limit of 20 minutes for preparation. During their presentations, encourage comments and questions from the rest of the group. If you have a multicultural class, ask individuals to prepare a short presentation at home to give within small groups or in front of the whole class, depending its size.

Extension activity: Read the Business across Cultures notes on page 153 of the Coursebook. If you did the extension activity on culture-specific words in the Business across Cultures section in Unit 10, ask students whether they would consider the Russians emotional or neutral. Why? What kinds of words or language do they use that demonstrate this?

Next, ask students to consider the behaviour of people in emotional (or 'affective') cultures and the behaviour of those in neutral cultures. To help them, suggest that they consider the following points:

body language   the sound of the voice   relationships
decision-making skills   expressing opinions

Divide the class into small groups and assign one culture to each group. Set a time limit of 5 minutes to brainstorm behaviour on flipchart paper. Elicit a couple of examples beforehand and circulate during the exercise to guide the discussion or make suggestions if necessary. When students present their ideas to the rest of the class, ask the other students to make comments and contribute further ideas.

Possible responses:

Emotional cultures

Ready to show feelings verbally and non-verbally.

Facial expressions show how people are feeling.

Gesture a lot.

Use intuition and feeling in making decisions.

Respect people who show their feelings and express their views openly.

May be quick to respond without having considered the facts in detail.

Focus on people more than tasks.

Physical contact (hugging, back-slapping, etc.) is acceptable.

Tend to use lively and melodic intonation.

Expressing emotions is seen as a way of releasing tension.

Neutral cultures

Keep emotions under control.

Appear reserved.

Showing your feelings is viewed as unprofessional.

Avoid physical contact (as it is considered taboo).

Calm behaviour is admired.

Don't express exactly what they are thinking.

Emotion should never influence objectivity in decision-making.

Tend to take time making decisions.

Focus on tasks more than people.

Tend to use monotonous intonation.

May 'bottle up' emotions and could explode.

When students have discussed and presented the behaviour of each culture, write the following nationalities on the board and ask students to match each nationality to a culture: *emotional, neutral,* or *a combination of the two cultures* (write these words on the board). It is a good idea to remind them that it is difficult to make generalisations about whole nations because behaviour is also a result of individual personality traits and the context people live in. However, there *are* national differences and analysing a culture means looking at the way people *generally* behave in certain contexts. This can be done as an open class discussion. Ask students to justify their views.

The French (a combination)	*The Americans (a combination – they are emotional but think it unprofessional to allow emotion to influence decision-making processes)*
The Italians (emotional)	*The Japanese (neutral)*
The Chinese (emotional)	*The Venezuelans (emotional)*

Ask students to work in pairs and discuss how they would describe their own culture and why. Allow up to 5 minutes for this then ask three or four students to summarise their discussions in front of the rest of the class.

Finally, instruct students to work out a set of rules for how each culture should behave or deal with the other in the following situations (write on the board):

Meetings and negotiations   Presentations

Assign one of the headings below to each group. Elicit one or two examples to check understanding of the exercise. Set a time limit of 5 minutes to brainstorm their ideas then ask them to present their ideas to the rest of the class.

Possible responses:

An 'emotional' in a neutral culture

Meetings and negotiations

Try to read between the lines.

Avoid making physical contact.

Agree to take time-out for reflection and assessment during meetings and negotiations.

Do not be offended if they seem reserved.

Remember that monotonous intonation does not mean they are bored or not interested.

<u>*Presentations*</u>

Try to 'contain' strong emotions during presentations.

<u>*A 'neutral' in an emotional culture*</u>

<u>*Meetings and negotiations*</u>

Be prepared for discussions that focus on <u>you</u> rather than the objective.

Remember that enthusiasm and excitement does not mean a decision has been made.

Try to be explicit when expressing your views. 'Emotionals' tend not to read between the lines.

<u>*Presentations*</u>

Try to work in a bit of intonation during presentations.

Try to appear enthusiastic.

▶ FOR FURTHER INFORMATION ON LATIN AMERICA SEE PAGE 58 OF THE WORKBOOK.

▶ REFER STUDENTS TO PAGE 153 OF THE COURSEBOOK FOR A SUMMARY OF THE POINTS COVERED IN THIS BUSINESS ACROSS CULTURES SECTION.

Checklist

Review the end of unit checklist items in the Coursebook with your students, as well as the unit word field. Add any interesting pronunciation items to the pronunciation file started in Unit 1.

Final activity: If appropriate for your class, look at one or two company annual income statements. These can be easily located on the Internet. Get the class to identify the sorts of expenses which might be included. Alternatively, ask your class to construct a simple profit and loss account on the board, if they have financial knowledge. Note that some terms will differ in American English. Explanations of financial terms and examples of financial accounts can be found at www.bizhelp24.com or in the book *Financial English* by Ian Mackenzie.

12 Escaping poverty

Reading and speaking
Vocabulary to enable students to discuss the challenges for developing economies, such as *financial services* and *corruption* is presented in this section.

Listening
In an interview with Sanjay Chakraborty, language for discussing the difficulties of getting out of the poverty trap, such as poverty line and microfinance, is tackled.

Grammar **reported speech**
Students learn to use a range of verbs for reporting speech.

Communication **negotiations 2: Handling conflict**
In this section students learn strategies for conflict resolution.

Business across Cultures **Africa**
This section examines African business culture and attitudes towards the law and the authorities.

Introductory activity

With Coursebooks closed, explain that the unit theme is escaping poverty. Ask the class to brainstorm a list of countries and continents which are caught in the poverty trap. Ask them to think of reasons why these countries may have difficulty getting out of this position. Answers might include: *Lack of education, health resources, unstable political situation, poor infrastructure.* Write all useful vocabulary up on the board.

Start-up

A Instruct the class to open their Coursebooks at page 82. Read the opening statement with the class. If necessary, pre-teach *get out of the way*. Find out what they think the statement really means and whether they agree with it. Answers might include: *help them to help themselves, give a man a fish, feed him for a day, teach a man to fish, feed him for a lifetime.*

Reading and speaking

A Ask the class to read the text and review all difficult or interesting new vocabulary, idioms and word combinations, such as, *hinder, inadequate, antiquated, abundance, volatility, sound education, stable future, impeded, help themselves to, obstructed, tariff barriers, development tools, extortionate, debt-ridden, collateral, acquire, bank loan,* and elicit synonyms explanations from the class. Start up a unit word field around the phrase *escaping poverty*. Encourage students to choose sub-categories around which to group new words. These might include: *causes of poverty, effects of poverty, financial terms.*

B Ask pairs to find words in the text to fit the definitions. Do a quick class answer check.

KEY
1 tariff
2 collateral
3 volatility
4 hinder / impede
5 an abundance
6 emigrate
7 accountable
8 extortionate
9 antiquated

C Ask pairs to discuss which of the factors in A and B are 'causes' of poverty, and which are 'effects'. They should make two lists. Divide pairs into two groups to discuss and compare their lists.

D Ask small groups to discuss how these problems can be dealt with and what can be done to pull people out of poverty. Get each group to present its ideas briefly and allow time for debate.
▶ VOCABULARY REVIEW AND DEVELOPMENT, PAGE 92 OF THE COURSEBOOK, CAN BE DONE AT THIS STAGE.
▶ FOR FURTHER READING AND VOCABULARY PRACTICE RELATING TO THE TOPIC OF POVERTY, DIRECT STUDENTS TO PAGE 59 OF THE WORKBOOK.

Listening

A Ask pairs to discuss the question briefly and report their conclusions back to the class. Add a sub-category for 'sources of finance' to the unit word field.

B AUDIO **12.1** Instruct the class to listen to the first part of an interview with Sanjay Chakraborty, a specialist in poverty reduction, and answer the questions individually. Do a class answer check.

KEY

1 They are hard to see.

2 Because they have no access to capital.

3 Microfinance.

4 In the mid-1970s in Bangladesh.

5 Women are more likely to reinvest their earnings in the business and in their families.

AUDIO SCRIPT

Interviewer: We all know that the global economy is racing ahead. China, India, and many other developing nations are growing very fast, and their booming economies are pulling millions of people out of poverty. But about half the world's population still lives on less than $2 a day. Here in the studio today is Sanjay Chakraborty, a specialist in poverty reduction from the organisation 'Power Over Poverty'. Good morning, Sanjay. Thank you for coming along today. Now, getting rid of global poverty is the most important economic and social challenge of our time. From your point of view, how can this be achieved?

Sanjay Chakraborty: Well, obviously, there is foreign aid. More than a trillion dollars of international aid, that's a thousand billion dollars, has been handed out in the last 50 years, but I would say that the results are hard to see.

Interviewer: Aha.

Sanjay Chakraborty: A more effective approach, in my opinion, is to encourage entrepreneurial activity among the poor, but of course, that requires finance, and traditional banks have not been willing to lend to poor people.

Interviewer: Ah, yes. As the famous economist Milton Friedman once said: the poor stay poor, not because they're lazy but because they have no access to capital.

Sanjay Chakraborty: That's right. And this has hindered progress in the developing world. In recognition of this fact, something called 'microfinance' has emerged to give poor people access to the precious capital they need to invest in their own projects or start up their own enterprises.

Interviewer: How and when did this start?

Sanjay Chakraborty: It was in the mid-1970s in Bangladesh. An academic called Muhammad Yunus had the idea of lending money to the very poor, particularly women. He set up a bank and called it the Grameen Bank Project, and it now has six million borrowers in over 64,000 villages. And 96 per cent of the customers are women.

Interviewer: 96 per cent? Why's that?

Sanjay Chakraborty: Because studies have shown that women are more likely to reinvest their earnings in the business and in their families, and they are more willing to be accountable. As families cross the poverty line and their businesses grow, the rest of their communities reap the rewards. Jobs are created, knowledge is shared, and women are recognised as valuable members of their communities.

C AUDIO **12.2** Ask the class to listen to the second part of the interview and answer the questions. Get pairs to compare their answers and do a quick answer check. Add useful phrases to the unit word field.

KEY

1 In microfinance, customers do not need collateral in order to receive a loan.

2 The rates in microfinance programmes often exceed those related to big business.

3 Because of the high loan repayment rates, and the enormous market potential in the large population of 'unbanked' poor.

4 Throughout the developing world, and even in poor communities in the developed world.

AUDIO SCRIPT

Interviewer: So, how does microfinance work?

Sanjay Chakraborty: Well, clients do not need collateral in order to receive loans. This allows people who would not usually qualify with traditional financial institutions to receive credit.

Interviewer: Wow. Does the bank make a profit? I mean it doesn't sound very profitable or secure.

Sanjay Chakraborty: Yes, the Grameen Bank has made a profit in every year of its existence except three. And the repayment rate for loans is 98 per cent. This is serious business, not charity. In fact, the repayment rates in many microfinance programmes often exceed those related to big business. Large banks and investors are increasingly viewing microfinance as a good opportunity because of the high loan repayment rates, and they have figured out that there is enormous market potential in the large population of 'unbanked' poor, particularly in India.

Interviewer: So, has the approach taken off in other parts of the world?

Sanjay Chakraborty: Yes, there is an abundance of microfinance lending institutions which have sprung up throughout Asia, Latin America, Africa, Eastern Europe, and elsewhere in the developing world, and even in poor communities in the developed world.

Interviewer: Aha.

Sanjay Chakraborty:	They come in all shapes and sizes: from small co-operatives that just take care of a few villages to giant companies spanning a nation. These institutions altogether have over 94 million customers.
Interviewer:	I see. So is microfinance the solution to beating global poverty?
Sanjay Chakraborty:	Microfinance alone will not stamp out global poverty, but it is having a significant impact. To illustrate this, a World Bank study showed that, in Bangladesh, Grameen Bank clients are escaping poverty at the rate of 10,000 per month.
Interviewer:	Well, that's quite impressive …

D Ask students to listen to both parts of the interview and write down the figures which correspond to the items in the exercise. Get individual students to read out their answers and do a number pronunciation check.

KEY

Proportion of world's population that live on less than $2 a day: more than half

Amount of international aid given to developing countries in the last 50 years: more than a trillion dollars

In relation to Grameen Bank:

Number of borrowers: 6 million

Percentage of women borrowers: 96 per cent

Rate of repayment of loans: 98 per cent

Number of customers using this form of finance worldwide: 94 million

Rate at which clients are escaping poverty: 10,000 per month

Speaking

Read through the opening statement and instruction with the class. Ask the class to work in pairs to prepare their short presentation. Ask the class to note down the unit language items used during each presentation and get them to give feedback after each presentation.

Grammar

Reported speech

A Read the rules for reported speech and model sentences with the class. Ask students to do the exercise as instructed in the Coursebook individually. Do a class review of answers.

KEY

1 He stressed that traditional banks had not been willing to lend to poor people.

2 He agreed that microfinance had emerged as a new approach to lending money.

3 He said that women were more likely to reinvest their earnings in the business.

B AUDIO 12.3 Tell the class to listen to ten statements and match each one to an appropriate reporting verb from the box, using each verb only once, then compare their answers with a partner.

KEY

1 replied   2 complains   3 explained   4 predicted
5 promises   6 added   7 confessed   8 denies
9 emphasised   10 warned

AUDIO SCRIPT

1 Yes. You're right. The loan was crucial in helping us to start a business and build up a future for our family.

2 It's not fair I'm in so much debt when the banks make huge profits.

3 A self-help group system means that a group works together to make an enterprise succeed.

4 I think that women in particular will benefit from the service for a long time to come.

5 I give you my word that everyone in the village will have access to a phone by the end of the year.

6 Not only that, but the bank runs several telephone and energy companies as well.

7 I admit that a lot of the money given in aid has been spent unwisely.

8 It's not true that poor people have a lower repayment rate for loans.

9 The repayment rate for loans is 98 per cent. Really, 98 per cent.

10 You must register your application by 1 December, or it will be too late.

C Read the rules and model sentences with the class. Ask pairs to listen again and take turns to report each statement back using the correct reporting verb. Pause the audio between each extract and allow pairs time to form an answer. Do a quick class answer check.

KEY

1 She replied that the loan had been crucial in helping them to start a business and build up a future for their family.

2 He complains that it isn't fair he is in so much debt when the banks make huge profits.

3 She explained that a self-help group system meant that a group worked together to make an enterprise succeed.

4 He predicted that women in particular would benefit from the service for a long time to come.

5 She promises that everyone in the village will have access to a phone by the end of the year.

6 He added that the bank ran several telephone and energy companies as well.

7 She confessed that a lot of the money given in aid had been spent unwisely.

8 He denies that poor people have a lower repayment rate for loans.

9 She emphasised that the repayment rate for loans was 98 per cent.

10 He warned us that we had to register our application by 1 December, or it would be too late.

D Ask the class to look at the questions from the interview with Sanjay Chakraborty and rewrite them in reported speech individually. Do a quick class answer check.

KEY

1 *He asked how and when this had started.*

2 *He asked how microfinance worked.*

3 *He asked whether / if microfinance was the solution to beating global poverty.*

E Ask your students to work in groups of four to do the exercise as indicated in the Coursebook. Do a last concept check if you hear any erroneous reported sentences.

▶ FOR FURTHER INFORMATION ON REPORTED SPEECH, REFER STUDENTS TO GRAMMAR OVERVIEW, PAGE 164 OF THE COURSEBOOK.

▶ FOR SELF-STUDY EXERCISES ON REPORTED SPEECH, SEE PAGE 60 OF THE WORKBOOK.

▶ GRAMMAR REVIEW AND DEVELOPMENT, PAGE 92 OF THE COURSEBOOK, CAN BE DONE AT THIS STAGE.

Communication

Negotiations 2: Handling conflict

A Read the opening statement with the class. Ask pairs to discuss the questions and report their answers back to the class briefly. They might prefer to report a conflict somebody else experienced. Answers might include: *Asked a superior to intervene / mediate, tried to discuss the problem rationally with the other party, the problem escalated, avoided doing anything about it.* Allow time for students to make suggestions about how to handle conflict situations and give examples of situations which were successfully resolved. Write any useful language up on the board.

B AUDIO **12.4** Read through the questions with the class. Check understanding of *customised accounting software solutions.* Get students to give an example of such a product. Play the audio and get students to answer the questions individually. Do a class answer check.

KEY

1 *The conflict is about who is responsible, Mastertons being unhappy and not paying for technical support.*

2 *Mastertons have to pay as they signed a contract with fixed payment terms.*

3 *He can't afford to upset them as they are his best client.*

4 *Take them to court to get the money.*

5 *Make them an offer.*

C Instruct students to look at the Key language box. Review any difficult expressions, such as, *sticking point, obstacle, in all our interests, to give some ground.* Get students to refer to the examples of conflict they gave at the beginning of the section and where possible, get them to describe these terms to the rest of the class. Ask them to listen again and identify the four points. Get a different student to explain each answer.

KEY

Use the audio script to check your answers.

AUDIO SCRIPT

Sean: It's not my fault, you know.

Helen: Well, it certainly isn't ours! Mastertons is your client and you introduced them to us. You're responsible for the contract and that includes payment. They've only been with us for six months and they've caused too many problems already!

Sean: OK, but it's your company that provides technical support and Mastertons aren't happy with the support they've received.

Helen: Sean, this is not going anywhere. Let's see where we are and where we can go. So, we know that Mastertons have refused to pay for technical support. Why exactly have they said this?

Sean: Basically, they say they're not paying for something they haven't received.

Helen: They haven't received the support because they haven't implemented the software fully. But, more to the point, we have a contract with fixed payment terms. They have to pay!

Sean: But Mastertons is one of my best clients. I can't afford to upset them.

Helen: Upset them! How do you think we feel about this? I'm sorry but they've got to pay up.

Sean: Well I think you'll have to go to court to get the money.

Helen: So, that's what we'll do. I'd like you to get that moving. Maybe they'll pay up when they see we mean business.

Sean: And meanwhile I will have lost a lot of other business with Mastertons and the prospect of any more in the future.

Helen: So what do you suggest?

Sean: Well, I think we need to make them an offer – you know – something positive. We need to find something in all our interests.

Helen: Like what?

Sean: Perhaps we can agree to forego payment on the support, on the basis that they buy one of your off-the-peg packages.

D Get students to work in pairs and do the exercise as indicated in the Coursebook. Remind them that their aim is to find some common ground in this negotiation and to use the Key language items where possible. If necessary, appoint an observer to each pair. Either way, ask students to report back to the class on how they reached a workable compromise. Encourage them to repeat the specific language they used. The Negotiation Feedback framework on page 126 can be used.

▶ FOR DEVELOPMENT AND CONSOLIDATION OF THE LANGUAGE ABOVE, SEE PAGE 62 OF THE WORKBOOK.

▶ REFER STUDENTS TO PAGE 14 OF THE COURSEBOOK FOR A SUMMARY OF THE POINTS COVERED IN THIS COMMUNICATION SECTION.

▶ COMMUNICATION REVIEW AND DEVELOPMENT EXERCISES, PAGE 93 OF THE COURSEBOOK, CAN BE DONE AT THIS STAGE.

Business across Cultures

Africa

Read the introduction together.

A Ask students to brainstorm the image they have of Africa in pairs. Compare their ideas in class.

B Instruct students to read the article individually then discuss the points in pairs. Compare responses in class.

C AUDIO **12.5** Play the audio more than once if necessary and do a class answer check.

KEY

1 *People don't trust official authorities any more.*

2 *People no longer believe that politicians can do anything for them, so they don't vote.*

3 *Business people cannot create wealth for the country. They can only create wealth for themselves by paying bribes which leads to inefficient allocation of resources.*

AUDIO SCRIPT

The thing about corruption is that it really undermines everybody's belief in a fair society. It undermines the rule of law and means that people don't trust official authorities. Some people avoid paying taxes because they can't see any benefit from paying them. Corruption also affects the political system as people no longer believe that politicians can do anything for them. So, many people don't vote because they don't believe in the system. In the business world, corruption affects competition. Businesses that play by the rules don't necessarily succeed. This means that they cannot create wealth for the country. People believe they can only create wealth for themselves by paying bribes. Corruption also results in the inefficient allocation of resources – very often the people who get the resources are the last ones who need them. Unfortunately, the poor get poorer and the rich get richer.

D Set a time limit of 5 minutes for the discussion. Afterwards, ask one person from each pair to summarise their views for the rest of the class.

E Get different students to read about each type of culture in front of the rest of the group.

You could tell them an anecdote based on your own experience or use the one below to check their understanding of the two cultures.

If you choose to use the anecdote below, first ask students what *jaywalking* is (it's a traffic offence in many countries and is committed by pedestrians when they cross the road outside a designated pedestrian crossing or when they don't adhere to traffic statutes). Next, tell students the anecdote:

I don't like the idea of not being allowed to cross the road when there is no danger. And I object to the assumption that the car is more important than the pedestrian. Why shouldn't I cross the road if it is clear? I remember waiting at a crossing by a railway station in Switzerland, together with some local people. There was not a car in sight, but as I walked across I heard someone shout 'The traffic light is red!' in German. She sounded really shocked!

Ask students to identify the universalist behaviour (the Swiss lady) and particularist behaviour (the narrator) in the anecdote. Ask why the Swiss lady might object to the jaywalking.

Possible responses:

The law applies to everyone.

If we all started crossing the road whenever we wanted, it would be chaos.

The law is there to protect people. What if a child witnessed the incident and started jaywalking? The child may get hit by a car.

How might the Jaywalker react to the situation?

Possible responses:

Why didn't any of the local people cross the road? It seems mindless to wait for the green light when there's no traffic. Very conformist!

I know it's against the law, but I crossed the road when it was safe. It depends on the circumstances, doesn't it?

People should trust themselves to make the right decision. After all, we're all responsible for our own safety.

Ask pairs to discuss which culture they belong to. Afterwards, get four or five students to summarise their discussions and give reasons for their conclusions.

F Ask students to do the exercise as indicated in the Coursebook. Afterwards ask students to share their ideas with the rest of the class.

As an extension to this exercise, you could ask students to look at each of the three business situations again and work out which of the two cultures (universalist or particularist) are portrayed. Get students to work in pairs then share their ideas with the rest of the class.

G Allow up to 10 minutes to discuss these statements. Afterwards, ask students to share their views with the rest of the class.

Extension activity: Put students into small groups and brainstorm the negative perceptions that universalists and particularists are likely to hold of each other. Assign one of the headings below to each group and allow up to 10 minutes to brainstorm perceptions on flipchart paper. Elicit a couple of examples beforehand and circulate during the exercise to guide the discussion or make suggestions if necessary. When students present their ideas to the rest of the class, ask the other students to make comments and contribute further examples.

A particularist's view of universalists

Uncompromising, rigid and inflexible. They think there is only one truth.

Unforgiving. After all, everyone makes mistakes.

Cold and inhuman. They focus more on rules than relationships.

Authoritarian.

Untrusting. They tend to focus on legal constraints rather than the individual or circumstances.

Rude and impersonal communication style.

You can't trust them because they don't even help their friends.

If you don't make exceptions, you weaken community and family ties.

Applying such strict principles to such a complex world is 'simplistic'.

They are insensitive to local conditions and culture. They think that what is appropriate in one place will work everywhere else.

Universalism is a kind of 'mindless formalism'.

<u>*A universalist's view of particularists*</u>

Corrupt.

No sense of 'fair play' or justice. If friends or family violate rules, it is OK in particularist cultures.

Lack common standards and rules to make sure that everyone is treated equally.

If you make exceptions, you weaken equality and order.

You can't trust them because they always help their friends.

How on earth can they implement a judicial system that is credible?

Legal contracts are meaningless in this culture.

They are vague and evasive. They hold too many views on reality and what is right.

They waste a lot of time making small talk (there's a strong focus on relationships as opposed to rules).

Particularists dodge responsibility (when confronted with a rule, they will argue that it doesn't apply to them).

Once students have presented their perceptions, you could then ask them to work out how universalists and particularists can deal with each other effectively. Once again, assign one of the headings below to each group. Set a time limit of 5 minutes to brainstorm their ideas then ask them to present their ideas to the rest of the class.

Possible responses:

<u>*How a particularist should deal with a universalist*</u>

To avoid being viewed as 'corrupt', try to respect the rules and guidelines as much as possible.

Do not be offended if they seem untrusting; they simply like <u>everyone</u> to stick to the rules.

Be prepared to justify any changes you wish to make to an agreed contract.

Do not take their formal approach as rude or cold.

Try to accept that one of the main aims of universalism is to achieve 'equality'.

<u>*How a universalist should deal with a particularist*</u>

Accept that what works in your own culture may not work elsewhere. Be sensitive to local conditions.

Accept that a contract may not be the last stage in a negotiation.

Be prepared for any modifications to the original contract.

Take time to nurture a relationship with your contact.

Accept that one of the main aims of particularism is to be loyal to one's friends and family.

Once students have shared their ideas, ask them if there are any rules that could be applied to both cultures. Do this as a whole class brainstorming exercise.

Possible responses:

<u>*Rules that apply to both universalists and particularists*</u>

Understand and respect any differences you observe.

Remember that both cultures are based on ethical principles: one adheres to equality through rules and the other promotes loyalty through putting relationships first. How we view these principles all depends on our cultural programming.

Try to find a compromise by establishing a formal contract which allows discretionary changes.

Remember that many people in such cultures may not conform to their cultural norms.

▶ FOR A READING ACTIVITY ON SOUTH AFRICA SEE PAGE 63 OF THE WORKBOOK.

▶ REFER STUDENTS TO PAGE 153 OF THE COURSEBOOK FOR A SUMMARY OF THE POINTS COVERED IN THIS BUSINESS ACROSS CULTURES SECTION.

▶ TO REVIEW THE DIFFERENT CULTURAL VALUES PRESENTED IN THE COURSEBOOK, REFER TO PHOTOCOPIABLE 3.3 ON PAGE 120.

Checklist

Review the end of unit checklist items in the Coursebook with your students, as well as the unit word field. Add any interesting pronunciation items to the pronunciation file started in Unit 1.

Final activity: Noun_noun linking intrusive /r/

Review the final activity on noun_noun linking and intrusive /w/ in Unit 10.

Put the following phrases on the board and ask the class to say them quickly.

prior_agreement   further_information   closer_alliance

Elicit that the intrusive sound /r/ can be heard in between the two words. Ask the class to review audio script 12.3 on page 125 in pairs. Ask one student to read sentences 1, 2, 4 and 10 quickly and the other student to mark in where they hear an intrusive /r/. In *most* British English accents the final /r/ in a word is not enunciated when no word follows it. In many American accents it is. In either form of English, an intrusive /r/ will join the two words, possibly making them difficult to distinguish for the student.

Listen to the audio again and do a class answer review. Intrusive /r/ may or may not appear, depending on the nationality and speaking style of the speakers. Whilst it is useful to know where this linking sound can occur when native speakers are speaking, it is not necessary for students to reproduce it at all times. However, if they can do this they will produce a more authentic sound and sentence stress pattern.

Possible occurrences of intrusive /r/

1 Yes. You're right. The loan was crucial in helping us to start a business and build up a future fo**r_o**ur family.

2 It's not fai**r_I**'m in so much debt when the banks make huge profits.

4 I think that women in particular will benefit from the service fo**r_a** long time to come.

10 You must register you**r a**pplication by December 1st, **or it** will be too late.

Business Scenario 3

Katabaro Hotel

Building on the theme of business in Africa, which is examined in Unit 12, this Business Scenario is set in Tanzania where the owner of a decaying luxury hotel is looking for an investor to return it to its former glory. In the negotiation exercise, students role play the negotiation between the hotel owner and a potential investor from Saudi Arabia. This gives students practice of the language of negotiating, which appears in Units 11 and 12. Students then hold a meeting to discuss the breakdown of costs for renovation of the hotel. This not only allows students to practise the language of meetings, which is presented in Units 9 and 10, but also provides an opportunity to use the language for talking about budgets, which appears in Unit 11. The writing exercise involves composing an email which summarises the outcome of the meeting.

With Coursebooks closed, ask the following question:

These days, many hotels make an effort to cater for business people. What facilities and services do they offer?

Ask students to brainstorm answers in pairs. Allow 5 minutes then ask them to share their ideas with the rest of the class. Write their answers on the board.

Possible responses:

Conference centres

Meeting rooms

Private offices

Business centres

Wireless high-speed Internet access

Tele-videoconferencing

High-speed duplicating, printing, scanning and document processing

Courier and administrative services

Audio-visual and presentation equipment hire

Technical support

Catering services

Organisation of corporate events

Background

Before reading the report, ask where Tanzania is and what students know about it. (It's on the Indian ocean on the east coast of Africa. It is home to Mount Kilimanjaro, Africa's highest mountain. It has many significant wildlife parks and is a growing tourist destination.)

Ask two students to read the newspaper report out loud in class. Deal with any vocabulary queries by asking students to provide definitions for each other then ask one student to summarise the report in his/her own words.

Negotiation

Read the introduction to the exercise together in class then ask students to form pairs. Draw students' attention to the Useful language, and, if you wish, elicit further negotiating phrases which appeared in the Communication sections of Units 11 and 12. Tell students to make an effort to use at least three of the expressions during the negotiation simulation.

Look at the breakdown of costs together. Check understanding of words like *renovation, ballroom, function,* and *to landscape.* Tell students that they will not need to refer to this table much during the negotiation; it will be used in a meeting activity later.

Assign roles to each person and ask students to turn to the relevant pages to study their roles. Tell them that you would also like them to start the meeting with a little bit of small talk as it is Mr Madani and Mr Macha's first meeting.

Allow 5 minutes for preparation and, during this time, help students if they have queries concerning vocabulary or context.

Set a time limit of 20 minutes for the negotiation. Circulate during the activity and make a note of negotiating language, active listening and general interaction. Provide feedback after the exercise and ask students:

Did you achieve your objectives during the negotiation? If so, how?

If not, why not?

Discussing a budget

Before looking at this exercise, it would be a good idea to review the language for leading and participating in meetings very briefly. Write *Leading meetings* on the board and ask students if they can remember what the *four Ps* are and why they are important:

Preparation

Purpose

Process

People

Next, write *Participating in meetings* on the board and ask: *Why is asking questions important in a meeting?* (It's an important way to participate and influence decisions.)

Then write the following headings on the board and elicit examples of questions (see the Communication section of Unit 10 for examples):

Clarifying

Reformulating

Showing interest

Leading

Seeking agreement

Suggesting action

Before the meeting, you may also wish to review the language used for describing budgets, which was presented in the Listening and Speaking section of Unit 11.

Read the introduction to the exercise together. Make sure that students understand that renovation of the main hotel building is essential, so $1,800,000 has already been spent.

Divide the class into groups of four and assign roles to each student. Ask a well-organised and reasonably confident student to play the role of Mr Macha, who will chair the meeting.

Allow students 5 minutes to prepare for their role. Longer may be necessary as students will have to study the breakdown of costs in relation to their role. They will also need to think of arguments for and against certain options. Warn students that they will need to take notes about any decisions made during their meetings as they will need this information to do the writing exercise below. Circulate during preparation to help with any queries concerning language or context.

Set a time limit of 20 minutes for the meeting. Run the meetings simultaneously and, if possible, record each one on audio to analyse during feedback. Students often find it useful to observe their own strengths and weaknesses. However, do not spend too much time listening to the recordings as students are likely to lose interest. Try to use them selectively to highlight positive interaction and elicit areas that could be improved. It is important to ask students for their opinions about the meeting: *Did you achieve the aim of the meeting? Is everyone satisfied with the results? Did everyone have a chance to speak? Did you understand each other?*

Writing

This could be set for homework. Ask them what could be mentioned in the email. For example:

Background and reason for the meeting

Participants and their opinions

Options discussed

Decisions (and reasons)

Correct their writing outside class then select some examples to use in class to highlight weaknesses and strengths common to the group.

Review and development 9–12

Vocabulary: A thriving economy

A This is best done individually or for homework.

KEY

1 port	2 thriving	3 pin down	4 spectacular
5 found	6 corridors	7 flourish	8 hang over

```
M  P  F  L  O  U  R  I  S  H  E  L  A  M
Y  I  O  P  E  C  N  Z  P  W  J  N  C  U
I  T  H  R  I  V  I  N  G  D  E  E  S  L
S  P  E  C  T  A  C  U  L  A  R  R  B  T
P  E  S  T  O  A  U  V  F  L  P  U  M  H
I  S  N  J  T  R  O  K  O  D  U  D  C  A
N  R  I  Y  H  F  R  K  U  Z  U  Y  E  N
D  P  Q  O  X  B  U  I  N  V  Y  N  T  G
O  X  A  C  U  A  Y  Q  D  P  D  A  A  O
W  U  L  P  L  H  A  N  G  O  V  E  R  V
N  S  F  C  C  P  L  Q  U  I  R  I  X  E
R  E  S  T  R  I  C  T  I  O  N  S  G  R
```

Grammar: Cause and effect

A This is best done individually or for homework.

KEY

1b due to

2c due to / because of / owing to / as a result of

3d because / as

4a because / as

5g so

6e therefore / consequently / as a result

7h results in

8f therefore / consequently / as a result

Vocabulary: Foreign investment

A This is best done individually or for homework.

KEY

1 money laundering   2 come into the equation

3 weigh up   4 inflation

Grammar: Referring and sequencing

A Again, this is best done individually or for homework.

KEY

1 These include   2 This is   3 First   Then   Finally

Vocabulary: Boosting the bottom line

A KEY

1 economic downturn	2 revenue	3 plummet
4 lay off 5 expenditure	6 stretch	7 overheads

B KEY

to dampen down

to bring down

to cut back on

to minimise

to cut

Grammar: Prepositions

A Again, this is best done individually or for homework.

KEY

1 in line with   2 In terms of   3 in view of

4 With regard to   5 beside the point

Vocabulary: Escaping poverty

A Ask students to do this task in pairs then compare answers in class. If students do not understand some of the words, get other students to provide definitions.

KEY

1 Strict tariffs <u>prevent</u> the free flow of goods between countries.

2 The educated <u>emigrate</u> for better opportunities abroad.

3 Extortionate world interest rates <u>force</u> third world countries to maintain impossible interest payments.

4 Poor infrastructure <u>hinders</u> development and progress.

5 Due to antiquated emergency mechanisms, the third world <u>suffers</u> more when natural disasters occur.

6 Awkward geographic features <u>slow</u> the spread of new technology.

7 An abundance of natural resources <u>brings about</u> market volatility.

8 Entrepreneurs <u>require</u> collateral to get a business loan.

9 Lack of accountability <u>encourages</u> corruption.

Grammar: Reported speech

Prior to the task, elicit as many reporting verbs as possible and write them on the board.

Possible responses:

say	tell	mention	inform	explain	admit
promise	deny	warn	complain	predict	confess
reply		emphasise		add	

Then write:

1 He   ?   <u>me</u> that he had seen the file.

2 He   ?   (<u>to me</u>) that he had seen the file.

Ask students which of the reporting verbs can be used with each sentence. Change the verbs to suit the sentence.

1 *told*   *informed*   *promised*   *warned*

2 *said*   *mentioned*   *explained*   *admitted*   *complained*   *confessed*
  predicted   *replied*   *denied*   *emphasised*   *added*

A Ask students to do the task in pairs then check answers in class.

KEY

1 *He argued that there was no evidence that microfinance ...*

2 *He promised that he would arrive on time for the meeting.*

3 *He complained that he hadn't received the report.*

4 *He admitted that he was capable of making mistakes and that he had invested in the wrong equipment.*

5 *He asked me whether poverty strengthened corruption.*

6 *He informed us that our company was too small to invest in.*

7 *He predicted that, by 2050, China, India, Brazil and Russia would probably be larger ...*

Extension activity: Ask students to watch an interview or short scenario, preferably with a business theme (this could be a clip from a current affairs programme or even a soap opera). While watching, students should make a note of things that were *said, mentioned, promised* and so on. Ask them to use the words on the board that were brainstormed earlier. Show the clip as many times as necessary, then ask students to tell you what happened. For example:

  She warned him that she would report him.

  He mentioned that he had worked for the company.

Communication

A Ask students to do this task in pairs then check their answers in class.

KEY

1e   2f   3a   4h   5c   6d   7b   8g

B Once again, ask students to do this task in pairs then check their answers in class.

Model answers

1 *Could you go over that again?*

2 *So, you're worried about the budget?*

3 *Could you tell me more about the budget?*

4 *Don't you think we should limit travel this year?*

5 *Does everyone agree that we should cut the budget?*

6 *What steps do we need to take?*

C Before embarking on this task, briefly review the different ways of describing conditions.

Examples:

  if   *provided that*   *so long as*   *on condition that*

Elicit example sentences for each.

Next, write the following on the board and elicit expressions:

  Acceptance

  Refusal + offer

Acceptance + condition

Rejection

(Further information can be found in the Communication section on page 79 of the Coursebook.)

Ask students to do task C in pairs then check answers in class.

KEY

Anna: So we have proposed our new prices. What do you think?

Matt: I'm afraid we can't agree to them.

Anna: I'm sorry to hear that. Would you consider them if we offered a quantity discount?

Matt: Perhaps. Provided the discount is across the full range of products.

Anna: That will be difficult as you do not buy some of the products in the right quantity.

Matt: Well, that may be so. But we can't go any further without an across-the-board discount.

Anna: We can't really agree to that but we could offer you a significant discount on your five main product categories.

Matt: That sounds interesting. What sort of discount?

Anna: Well, as long as you can guarantee minimum orders, we could offer a 15 per cent discount linked to early payment.

Matt: That could be interesting for us. Can you put this in writing?

D Ask students to do the task in pairs then compare their answers in class.

KEY

1 *difficulty*   2 *sticking point*   3 *propose*   4 *middle way*
5 *shared interest*   6 *option*   7 *answer*   8 *offer*

Elicit negotiating phrases that include these words.

For example:

  The main sticking point / difficulty / obstacle is ...

  What do you propose?

  That's the best offer I can make.

  One option / solution would be to...

  We need to find some common ground.

Writing resource

MODULE OVERVIEW

AIMS AND OBJECTIVES

This section is a resource which gives students further practice in emails, short reports and press releases. It also provides reading practice and some model examples. Each unit in this section relates to the theme and language of one of the three modules in logical order, so it is advisable to begin each one only after students have covered the relevant module. Units 14 and 15 relate specifically to the Business Scenarios for Modules 2 and 3, so these should be tackled before embarking on the Writing Unit.

PEDAGOGICAL NOTES

Each unit includes introductory or follow-up activities which are linked to the information and questions. Oral activities to elicit relevant vocabulary and ideas are suggested. Usually a particular type of exercise exploitation is suggested (e.g. individual, pairs, or class). Most *open* writing exercises are suggested as individual (possibly homework) exercises. Where possible it could be useful to ask students to submit these items of work, for review by yourself, before the next lesson. As with any other exercise in the Coursebook, adaptation of the writing exercises to the students' own work / study situation would be beneficial from the point of view of relevance and student motivation.

Before embarking on this module, review the differences between letter writing and emailing formalities. Elicit that in emails, the degree of formality is generally less formal than in a traditional business letter, particularly in opening and closing salutations. In appropriate situations more formal letters can be sent in email form and should still follow formal letter writing conventions. A review of the differences between reported and direct speech would also be useful, as well as linking phrases for lengthy texts.

UNIT 13: Developing people

This unit follows the Module 1 theme of people and people development. It prepares students for emails of enquiry about products and services, relevant to both pre-experience and work-experienced learners. It could be useful to review related items such as the vocabulary relating to teams and leaders in the first two units of the module. Students are asked to read and answer comprehension questions about an advertisement promoting corporate training services. They are then provided with a model email of enquiry about these services, into which they have to insert the correct letter of enquiry phrases. Students should develop an awareness of the overlap between formal letter writing

and emailing formalities in this context. This provides them with a basis on which to write their own email of reply. A model answer is provided to help review. A follow-up activity consisting of an authentic email of enquiry to a website is suggested. This should appeal to both work-experienced and pre-work learners.

UNIT 14: Local partners

This unit follows the Module 2 theme of markets and relates directly to the Module 2 Business Scenario, as well as getting students to practise determiners and quantifiers, presented on page 36 of the Coursebook. Students are asked to complete a model follow-up business report to a business meeting to decide on the overseas marketing strategy for a cycle company, with the correct determiners and quantifiers. This provides them with a model on which to base their own follow-up report to Aarit Motala, following their business scenario meeting with him. A final activity gets students to rearrange a series of sentences to complete an email from him, formally engaging their company as local partners.

UNIT 15: Getting away from it!

This unit relates directly to the Module 3 Business Scenario about the reopening of the Katabaro Hotel in Tanzania, as well as asking students to practise examples of direct and reported speech in the writing of a press release. Students are presented with a model press release about a similar hotel reopening. After reading it, they do a direct and reported speech exercise to focus on the grammatical changes which occur between the two forms, as well as using reporting speech phrases. Students then complete a gap-fill exercise, describing Tanzania, to build up relevant vocabulary in order to write their own press release for the Katabaro Hotel. A follow-up activity is suggested in the form of a radio broadcast of their press release, to emphasise the difference between the two forms of speech.

The Writing Feedback framework on page 127 can be used at any stage.

13 Developing people

- an advertisement for corporate training services
- an email requesting further information
- an email providing further information

Start-up

Tell the class that they are going to work on emails relating to an advertisement for corporate training services. Find out if any of your class have attended corporate training sessions. Ask questions such as: *Which types of corporate training service are likely to be provided by external providers? Why do companies buy in training services? What are the advantages and disadvantages of outsourcing them?*

Email exchange

A Ask students to read the advertisement. Do a quick review of any problematic vocabulary items.

B Ask the class to re-read the advertisement and to decide whether the statements in the exercise are true or false. Do a class answer check.

KEY

1 F They are under enormous pressure.

2 T

3 T

4 F They will coach the team before a presentation.

5 F They work with both public and private sector organisations.

C Review the phrases with the class and ask students to use them to complete the email to Renate Lenze, individually. Do a class answer check of the final email. Attention should be focused on the overlap of relatively formal letter writing (greeting salutation) and slightly less formal emailing conventions (closing salutation) in this email.

KEY

1 I am writing with reference to

2 Due to

3 we've realised that we urgently need

4 I'd be grateful if you could

5 I'm particularly interested to know

6 and roughly how many

7 It would also be extremely useful

8 I look forward to hearing about

9 Please don't hesitate to contact me

D Review the information given in the exercise with the class and ask students to write Renate Lenze's reply to Brian Owen's email, individually. This could be set as a homework activity. If necessary, correct each student's work individually, and do a class review of the model answer as well as any alternative phrases students used.

Model answer

To: brianowen@mediaco.co.uk_
Subject: RE: Enquiry about programmes
Date: 14 July 20____

Dear Brian,

Thank you for your enquiry regarding Dream Team Coaches. In answer to your questions about our coaching programme:

- our coaching sessions can be delivered in groups or on a one-to-one basis
- this can take place either at our corporate coaching centre in Swindon, or on your company premises
- distance coaching via email / telephone / Internet download is also available

Costs vary greatly depending on the nature and length of the training. However, to give you an idea of our standard prices, an all inclusive one-week residential group course at our coaching centre costs £3,000.

I have attached our company brochure which will give you further details about our programmes and facilities, including photos.

I hope I have been of some help. Please don't hesitate to contact me if you have any further queries.

Best regards,

Renate Lenze

Extension activity: Ask students to find a website advertisement (in English) for a product or service they are interested in and get them to write an email to the company to make further enquiries. Remind students to use relevant vocabulary from the advertisement in their email. They should print out the relevant website pages, a copy of their email, and a copy of the reply (which they are very likely to receive within 24 hours). If necessary, do an individual review of each student's emails. Then do a class review, in which students explain the product or service they were interested in and read out both their enquiry and reply to the class, whilst the students note down typical emailing phrases used. Alternatively, after each student has explained the nature of their enquiry, the rest of the class could be asked to guess the phrases each student used and received in their reply. Review any useful language items.

14 Local partners

- two business reports
- an email of confirmation of engagement

Introductory activity

Review the activities covered in the Business Scenario section on page 58 of the Coursebook with the class.

Start-up

Elicit that meetings are generally *followed up by* a report, based on the *minutes* taken during the meeting. Explain that this exercise aims to help students write a follow-up business report to that activity (as well as practise the use of determiners and quantifiers presented on page 36). Read the opening statements with the class.

A Ask the class to complete the exercise, individually. Do a class review of answers. Include a review of the *linking* and *cause and effect* expressions which are presented in the report, and ask the class to quickly brainstorm a few more such as: *although, therefore, whilst, whereas, due to, consequently.*

KEY

1 several   2 the   3 some of   4 few
5 the   6 a   7 this

B If necessary, ask your class to get back into the groups they formed to hold their meeting with Aarit Motala in the Business Scenario activity. Ask each group to briefly review the notes made during that meeting. Read the instructions with the class and ask them to do the exercise as instructed in the Coursebook. Remind students to use as many as they can of the linking and cause and effect expressions they brainstormed earlier in their report. This could be done as a homework activity and reviewed individually with each student, before a class review of report form and linking and cause and effect expressions, using the model answer.

Model answer

Dua Cycle Range advertising campaign
Summary
Aarit Motala, CEO of Dua, asked the Sharp Edge Cycles marketing team to attend a meeting to decide on a powerful marketing strategy for the Dua cycle product range to be launched in India. He asked the team to come up with a variety of original marketing ideas to present at the meeting. The following short report describes the Indian market background, the current level of competition and the final agreed marketing strategy for each product.

Introduction
The following points were considered:
- Local market
- Competitive environment
- Product range
- Product range image
- Product range marketing strategy

Local market
Young Indians prefer to shop online, are extremely brand conscious and are attracted to big foreign brands. Health and fitness, music, coffee bars and shopping malls are some of their main interests. Although there has so far only been one big mountain biking rally organised in India, leisure cycling has started to become quite fashionable in India and is seen as an eco-friendly alternative to driving.

Competitive environment
Although many high-end bicycles are manufactured in India, the range offered on the Indian market is very limited.

Product range
Mountain bike
BMX bike
Tour bike
Dua sportswear range

Product range image
Due to the growing trend towards health and fitness and outdoor pursuits, it was decided that the emerging Indian youth alternative sports lifestyle would be the main focus of the brand image.

Product range marketing strategy
Whilst the mountain bike will be advertised via mobile phones, the tour bike should be promoted in co-operation with the cycling holiday industry. Whereas the BMX bike would be best promoted through Bollywood product placement, sponsorship of student cultural and sporting events would be the most appropriate method of promotion for the sportswear range.

Conclusion
Analysis of the Indian cycling trends for the last few years shows that whilst this market is still relatively small, interest in cycling is on the increase. Dua is a highly successful established European brand which will be well received by the Indian youth market who have an appetite for quality foreign brands.

C Explain that after a successful meeting with Sharp Edge Cycles, and that having received the follow-up report, Aarit Motala wishes to engage them as local distributor. Read the instructions with the class and ask pairs to complete the exercise as indicated in the Coursebook. Get them to compare answers with another pair and do a class answer check, using the model answer as a guide.

KEY

Dear Amit, Shalina and Ira,

Firstly, let me congratulate you on our successful meeting two days ago. I was very impressed with your imaginative suggestions for marketing our Dua cycle range. I'm extremely pleased with the outcomes we arrived at, and am confident that with your expert local knowledge, Dua Cycles will be a success in India. Therefore, I'm pleased to confirm that I would be happy to sign an exclusive, five-year distribution contract with Sharp Edge Cycles.

Secondly, I'm keen to get this project underway as soon as possible, so I'd be grateful if you could start organising the marketing campaign immediately. Could you also send me a progress report by the end of next month?

Finally, once again, many thanks for all your energy and hard work. I look forward to a strong and profitable partnership between our companies in the near future.

Kindest regards,

Aarit Motala

To review the language in Units 7 and 14, refer to photocopiable 2.2 on page 115–116.

15 Getting away from it!

- Two press releases
- a description of a holiday location

Start-up

With Coursebooks closed, briefly review the Business Scenario section for Module 3 on page 88 with the class. Remind students of their meetings to decide on the refurbishment plan for the Katabaro Hotel. Elicit different ways of publicising the reopening of a holiday resort. Answers might include: *magazine ad with enticing photos, press releases, grand opening ceremony.* Explain that students are going to practise writing press releases in order to announce the reopening of the Katabaro Hotel to the international press and that they will review the use of reported speech, practised on page 84.

Press releases

A Ask the class to read the press release about the opening of The Royal in Sharm El-Sheikh. Do a quick class check of vocabulary and quickly elicit those numbered sentences which use reported speech and those which use direct speech, if necessary. Review the effect of reported speech on verb tense and the phrases used to bring some variety and impact to reported speech, such as: *proudly stated, announced.*

B Ask the class to do the exercise as instructed in the Coursebook, individually. Do a class answer check.

KEY

1 *Mr Abbas announced, 'The refurbishment will put the hotel back on the international luxury tourism map.'*

2 *He proudly stated that they already had bookings from a large number of world famous celebrities.*

3 *He went on to say 'it is not difficult to see why'.*

4 *He added, 'at all hours of the day and night, Sharm's legendary promenade, which stretches from one end of the bay to the other, is one of the country's most romantic strolling spots'.*

5 *'However, for diving enthusiasts', he continued, 'the real attraction lies beneath the surface of the crystal blue waters of the Red Sea.*

6 *He boasted that the exquisite guest rooms, as well as the hotel's unrivalled 18-hole golf course, club house and spa would provide the ultimate in restfulness and pampering.*

7 *He concluded that he was extremely proud to be the owner of one of the finest hotels in the world.*

C Ask students to do the exercise as instructed in the Coursebook, individually. As a class review, get one of your students to read out the text to the class, as if they were reading a radio report on the wonders of Tanzania.

KEY

1 *most picturesque*

2 *perfect place*

3 *very successful*

4 *extremely diverse*

5 *astounding*

6 *greatest concentration*

7 *second deepest*

D Ask the class to get back into the groups they formed to negotiate the refurbishment project for the Katabaro Hotel. Ask each group to review the email they wrote on decisions they made about the refurbishment before producing a group press release. Alternatively, after the group review, set the press release as an individual homework exercise. Review the individual or group press releases using the model answer as a guide if necessary.

Model answer

Today in Dar es Salaam, the spectacularly refurbished five-star Katabaro hotel, once regarded as one of the most classically luxurious hotels in the world, was reopened after a one-year refurbishment project costing over $4m. Investor Ibrahim Madani and owner Mr Macha were joined by a large number of world famous guests to reopen the hotel.

In his opening speech, Mr Madani announced, 'We already have bookings from a large number of high profile guests, including minor royalty and world famous business tycoons.'

He went on to say that it was easy to see why. 'The hotel is first class and situated in some of the most breathtaking scenery a holiday maker could wish for!' Home to the exotic islands of Zanzibar and Pemba, and with an exciting and diverse wild animal population, the luxury safari industry was already very profitable for the region. 'What is more, I don't think any other country can provide such a high number of astounding natural features!', he boasted. 'Tanzania is home to the largest crater in the world. For divers and anglers, Lake Tanganyika, the longest and second deepest lake in the world, is a paradise, with over 350 species of fish.' Whether you are keen on water sports or just enjoying the wonderful relaxation of the hotel's health and beauty spa and romance of its legendary giant ballroom, Tanzania is one of the most idyllic vacation spots in the world.'

'I am extremely happy to be the owner of one of the finest hotels in the world!', he proudly stated.

Extension activity: Ask pairs to make radio broadcasts of their own press releases. These could be performed live in front of the class or audio recorded and played back to the class. One student should play the part of reporter and the other should play the part of Mr Madani, so that the direct speech and reported speech parts are spoken by different students.

Photocopiable resource

INTRODUCTION

MODULE 1
People

1.1 is designed to get students thinking about, discussing and describing in writing, core vocabulary items, including multi-word and idiomatic expressions presented in Units 1 and 2, before engaging in a vocabulary guessing competition against other teams. Divide the class into two groups. Give each group a different vocabulary set. Ask groups to review the units to which their card relates. Ask each group to brainstorm and write a set of clues for these words. Encourage students to personalise their clues wherever possible as this will add interest and aid memory. This could be done as a homework activity and corrected before the lesson. If necessary, mingle and review accuracy with each group.

Sample sentences, charismatic: *this type of leader is loved by his / her employees and inspires them to work hard*; to gel as a team: *team bonding events aim to help groups of people who don't know each other very well to …*

Teams should take it in turns to read out their clues and award a point to the first team to produce the correct answer.

1.2 is designed to supplement the discussions about leadership and leadership styles and modal forms practiced in Unit 1. It also asks students to complete conditional sentences presented in Unit 3. Divide the class into small groups. Distribute a set of leadership style description cards to each group. Ask each student to read out one or more of the descriptions of leadership styles and get their group to complete the descriptions with the correct verb forms. Ask them to check their final answers with someone from another group and do a class answer check. Next, give each group a set of leadership style title cards and start a race to see which team can be first to correctly match up descriptions to titles.

KEY

Autocratic leadership – Our boss is like a dictator! If he had been more democratic in the last few years, employee turnover wouldn't have been so high. He should give us some opportunities to make suggestions and contribute ideas.

Bureaucratic leadership – If we didn't always have to do everything 'by the book', we could come up with more creative business solutions. We're in a very competitive business sector and should be allowed more flexibility.

Charismatic leadership – I don't know what would happen if our CEO left the company. We totally rely on his enthusiasm and energy to drive the business. Perhaps he should encourage the team to develop their skills a bit more in the future.

Democratic leadership – Our annual employee satisfaction surveys show that encouraging team members to contribute to the decision-making process has developed their skills and increased their motivation. If they didn't have this opportunity they might be more concerned about pay rises.

Laissez-faire leadership – Our team is highly experienced and we're generally just left to 'get on with it'. Our boss doesn't have to be looking over our shoulders all the time. So, if she needs to be brought up to date on a project, we give her a project progress presentation.

People-oriented leadership – Our last project manager was just like one of the team. If he had not been so supportive of our work and focused on developing us both as individuals and as a team, I don't think we would have achieved such a strong creative collaboration. We really should have nominated him for the 'boss of the year' award before he retired.

Task-oriented leadership – Our boss only ever focuses on targets and 'getting the job done'. If she wasn't constantly checking up on us, she might have more time to focus on the welfare and motivation of our team. She should be careful as she's having difficulties in retaining staff.

Transformational leadership – Our president inspires our team constantly with a shared vision of the future. She's always available to talk to employees and joins in a lot of meetings between junior staff. If she left the company, we would be unlikely to get another president like her. However she does have to be supported by a lot of 'details people'.

1.3 can be used after the Business across Cultures section of Unit 3. The aim of this activity is to demonstrate how cultural differences influence cross-border communication and to provide students with the opportunity to 'experience' culture clash through a simulation. It will take approximately two hours so you may need to do it over two sessions. There are three stages to this activity and it is recommended that stages two and three be done within the same session.

Stage 1: Refer students to the Business across Cultures notes relating to Unit 3 on page 151 of the Coursebook. Read through the three sets of values then divide the class into three groups. Assign each group the task of brainstorming the behaviour and attitudes they would expect within *two* of the value groups.

Ask students to present their ideas to the rest of the class. If they don't include the following points, try to elicit them:

Masculine	**Feminine**
Assertive/Interrupt a lot	Value relationships
Ambitious/Competitive	Sympathetic/Supportive
Task-oriented	Seek harmony/Take turns to speak
Materialistic	More accepting of women in management

High-power distance	**Low-power distance**
Subordinates do not challenge their superiors	Subordinates are involved in decision-making
Boss is autocratic	Boss is democratic

High-context	**Low-context**
Indirect, even ambiguous	Direct and to the point
Listening is important	Look to words used for understanding
Look to the context for understanding	Go into a lot of detail during discussions
Don't discuss background information	

Stage 2: Divide the class into four groups. Set the scene by telling them that they now inhabit a different world, with countries with names like Bravadia and Placidia. Tell students that each group represents a different 'country team' of the global Internet giant 'E-xplore', which provides a free Internet search engine. Hand out the information slips to each team and tell them to read them carefully.

Next, ask each team to discuss their 'culture' and work out how they should behave as Bravadians, Placidians and so on. Limit this discussion to five minutes.

Task 1: Make sure that students elect a team leader in accordance with their culture. For example, if they are from a masculine culture, they are unlikely to have a female leader.

Task 2: Once again, stress the importance of carrying out the meeting in a style that conforms with their cultural values and expectations. For example, in a low-context culture they will be direct with each other and in high-power distance culture the boss is likely to dominate. Allow 10 minutes for the meeting.

Stage 3: Once each team has decided on a strategy, tell them that they are now going to meet their counterparts in other countries to try to agree on a strategy. Write the names of the countries on the board and ask the Bravadian delegation to meet the Placidians, and the Tacitalians to meet the Bluntlunders. Remind students that they must continue to communicate in a way that is appropriate to their culture. Allow a maximum of 10 minutes then repeat the task by putting the Bravadians with the Bluntlunders and the Placidians with the Tacitalians.

Stage 4: Debrief

Ask each group to spend approximately 15 minutes discussing the following questions:

1. Did the first meeting (within your own team) go well? Why? Why not?
2. Describe the cultures of the two 'foreign' teams that you met. How did their communication style differ from that of your 'own culture'?
3. Did those cross-border meetings go well? Why? Why not?
4. Which culture was closest to your 'own'?

Finally, bring the class together, asking each group to briefly summarise their discussion. Did they identify the 'foreign' teams' values (i.e. masculine, low power distance etc.)? Ask students if they experienced 'culture clash'. If so, what can they do to avoid culture clashes in real life? Make a note of students' suggestions on the board.

MODULE 2

Markets

2.1 should be used just before task H in the Business across Cultures section of Unit 5.

The aim of this activity is to introduce students to the concept of monochronic and polychronic cultures and how challenges can arise when the two cultures meet.

Prior to this lesson, the teacher may wish to read the Business across Cultures notes relating to Unit 5 on page 152 of the Coursebook for some background information.

For further information and some excellent business anecdotes relating to polychronic and monochronic cultures, see the following website: www.zmk.uni-freiburg.de/ss2000/texts/gesteland(e).htm

Stage 1: Do not tell students what the aim of this activity is or mention monochronic and polychronic cultures. They will analyse the role plays later and identify the two cultures.

Divide the class into groups of three and assign roles to each person: an architect and a client, and the third student will observe the scenario.

Allow students plenty of time to read their roles. Warn them not to show their roles to anyone else. Circulate and help students if they have any queries regarding vocabulary or context. Remind the 'architects' and the 'clients' that they should do their best to achieve their aims during the meeting (to create a real sense of pressure, tell them that the observer's job is to record who is most successful in achieving their aims). Make sure that the observers do not divulge what is really on their checklist.

Tell students that you would like them to complete the meeting within the time stated on their role card. Circulate and make a note of any interesting points, particularly relating to those on the observer's sheet. Also make a note of any emotions and their causes (e.g. *Pablo seemed confused when Marta left the room. / Juhani was obviously frustrated when there wasn't much time left to discuss the agenda*).

Stage 2: Instruct the teams to discuss their meetings. Ask the observers to use their notes to provide feedback to the other team members and ask the 'architects' and the 'clients' to describe their feelings (*surprised, satisfied, stressed, confused, etc.*) at different stages of the meeting and why they felt that way.

Allow about five minutes for this discussion then begin a whole class discussion.

Ask the architects:

How did you feel during the meeting? Why?

Write their responses on the board as shown below:

Architects

Stressed ➜ *Wanted to get on with the agenda. Client kept making small talk.*

Annoyed ➜ *There were lots of time-wasting distractions.*

Surprised ➜ *Client didn't take schedules and deadlines seriously.*

Then ask the clients the same question and write their responses on the board:

Clients

Annoyed ➜ *Wanted to make small talk but architect was very focused on discussing business.*

Stressed ➜ *Didn't achieve my objectives.*

Ask the observers if they noticed anything else.

Next, ask students if they can describe the behaviour of the two people. Write their ideas on the board.

Possible responses:

Architect	*Client*
Time focused	Doesn't care about time
Focuses on task	Focuses on relationships
Focuses on one thing at a time	Does many things at once
Likes to stick to plans	Changes plans easily

Instruct students to read the Business across Cultures notes relating to Unit 5, page 152 of the Coursebook. Ask them which cultures the architect (monochronic) and client (polychronic) probably come from.

Stage 3: Finally, ask students to get into small groups and brainstorm how the two cultures can work effectively together. Allow five minutes for this then ask students to share their ideas with the rest of the class.

Possible responses:

Do your homework before meeting a foreign business person. Find out about their culture so that you are prepared.

Remember that there is more than one way of achieving your objectives. Use the approach that best fits the local circumstances.

Monochronic cultures should schedule in more time for a meeting with polychromic counterparts.

Polychronic cultures should be aware that interruptions and distractions during meetings may make monochronic counterparts feel uncomfortable.

Both cultures may need to accept that they do not share the same aims and try to find a compromise.

2.2 reflects the module theme of markets and review and practise phrases are used to make more accurate comparisons in Unit 7, as well as some of the linking phrases in Unit 14 for contrasting purposes. This activity can be done after Units 7 and 14 have been tackled. After a review of the relevant items in Units 7 and 14, divide the class into groups of three. Distribute A, B and C country statistics sheets. Ask students to provide their partners with information about the country on their sheet and ask for statistics relating to the other two countries. Students should check, clarify and read back information to make sure they have taken it down correctly.

Tell students that where possible they should use as many as they can of the modifying expressions from Unit 7. Model a sample exchange if necessary.

Example exchange:

Student A: How big is Russia's population?

Student C: It's one hundred and forty two point eight nine million.

*A: Ah! China's population is **a great deal bigger**, at one point three one billion!*

*C: So is India's population **bigger than** that?*

*B: No, not quite. It's **far bigger than** Russia's population, but at one point one billion, it's **slightly smaller than** that of China.*

Equally, linking (contrast) expressions such as: *whereas, whilst, although*, practised in Unit 14 can be used to make some of the country comparisons more interesting.

Example exchange:

Student C: Who are China's main import partners?

*Student A: They are Japan, at 15.2 per cent, closely followed by South Korea and Taiwan, at **just over** 11 per cent each. Who are India's main import partners?*

*B: Well, **whereas** China imports mainly from the ..., India's main import partners are China and the US. What about Russia?*

*C: Actually, Russia's import partners are Germany and the Ukraine, **although** Japan and China export **nearly as much as** the Ukraine to Russia.*

2.3 practises the grammar component of Unit 8, discussing future probabilities. Put students into pairs and distribute the A and B predictions cards. Tell students they should introduce each prediction on their card with the words: *By 2030 ...* Their partner should agree or disagree with each statement, using the unit key language, giving reasons to support their answer where possible. When students have completed the exercise, tell students to sit in two groups: Students A and Students B. Get them to compare their ideas and find out which was the most popular opinion about each statement. Groups should report the most popular opinions in a class review.

MODULE 3
Money

3.1 gives students further practice in using the cause and effect expressions they studied in Unit 9 and the referring and sequencing linkers from Unit 10. Using this language, students are asked to summarise some of the issues from Unit 10. Put students into pairs and give out a linking phrases card to each student. Give students time to prepare statements on their topic using the linking phrases to link the information on their topic card into logical sentences. Students should feel free to input ideas and vocabulary where they can. If you think students might need more time to do this, set it as a homework activity. Provide individual correction before asking students to explain their topic to their partner.

Possible sentences:

Student A
Foreign direct investment is an important means for helping developing economies to grow. Due to heavy foreign investment in new and expanding businesses, China and India are enjoying fast growth of their economies. As a result, many of their citizens are benefitting from increased prosperity.

Student B
There are a number of potential risks to avoid when considering foreign direct investment. The first thing is the question of emerging but incomplete democracies. These might suffer from political and economic instability. Related to this there is the risk that their governments might take back control of inward investors' subsidiaries or entire industries in which foreign companies have invested heavily. Consequently, a foreign investor could lose expensive assets.

3.2 aims to review and practise contractions and their role in intonation and stress patterns, which have an impact on the meaning of a sentence. Before embarking on this activity, write up the sentence, *Great! You are on the right track!* Ask pairs to say this sentence, quickly and naturally. Elicit that this would be spoken as *Great! You're on the right track!* Then write up the phrase *Ah! There you're!* Elicit that this should be spoken *Ah! There you are!* Ask pairs to read and rewrite the audio script together, contracting words where it makes the rhythm of the sentence more natural and using full forms where appropriate. Finally, ask pairs to underline the stressed words in each sentence. Get one or two pairs to role play their scripts to the class. Encourage the class to contribute suggestions. Listen to audio 12.4 as a class check. Elicit that auxiliaries and modals are often contracted so that the emphasis falls on the main verb. Where they are not contracted, this often means that it is necessary to stress one of the words in the contracted phrase because it is important in its context. For example:

And meanwhile I will have lost a lot of other business with Mastertons and the prospect of any more in the future. In this sentence the *I* is emphasised, so it stands alone from *will*.

The objective of **3.3** is to review the different cultural values and norms that have appeared in the Business across Cultures sections of the Coursebook.

Before embarking on this activity, elicit the different types of cultures that you have examined over the course (e.g. high and low context, monochronic and polychronic, collectivist, face-saving, etc.) and put them on the board for students to refer to during the first task.

Task 1: Ask students to work in pairs, preferably with someone from a different culture. Give each person a copy of the sheet and tell them that it features eight cultural values, assumptions or concepts that are perceived as 'common sense' somewhere in the world.

Ask students to look at each one (instruct them to ignore the lines at this stage as you will deal those later) and answer the following questions:

> *In which cultures might you find these views?* (Tell students that they can refer to the cultures written on the board.)
> *Why might people hold these views?*

Allow students up to 10 minutes to discuss these questions then ask them to share their ideas in class.

Possible responses:

1 *Typical in cultures that strongly believe in saving face.*
2 *Relates to monochronic and polychronic cultures. This particular value is common among Arab businessmen who believe God is the only one in control of the future.*
3 *Typical in a low-context culture where people rely completely on verbal cues for understanding.*
4 *Commonly held belief in individualistic cultures.*
5 *Common in cultures where there are closed inner circles.*
6 *Some cultures, particularly collectivist cultures, are strongly opposed to boasting and flaunting one's achievements.*
7 *Common perception in reserved cultures.*
8 *Typical feeling in task-oriented cultures.*

Task 2: Next ask students to discuss the following questions with their partner:

> *Which values / assumptions do you agree with? Which do you disagree with? Why?*

Ask four or five students to tell you about their views on one or two values.

Task 3: Ask students to change partners. Again, if possible, get students of different nationalities to work together. Instruct them to look at their sheets again and draw their attention to the two horizontal lines below each statement. Explain that you want them to write two alternative values / assumptions for each statement by changing the text in *italics*. Elicit an example to demonstrate the task. Allow up to 10 minutes for this then ask students to share their ideas in class.

Possible responses:

1 Showing annoyance in a negotiation *is OK because you shouldn't hide your feelings.*
   might cause <u>you</u> to lose face.

2 Trying to see into the future and form rigid deadlines *is obviously good planning.*
   prevents you from being flexible.

3 Directness, openness and honesty *should be avoided if you want to preserve harmony.*
   are naïve and childish forms of behaviour.

4 Educational institutions *should not allow their students to challenge the lecturers.*
   should teach young people how to collaborate and cooperate.

5 Strangers *should always be treated with respect and made welcome.*
   should be treated with suspicion.

6 Standing out from the crowd *is something to be proud of. It's an objective!*
   is non-conformist.

7 When people speak loudly and gesture a lot, *they are trying to get their message across.*
   they are expressing enthusiasm.

8 Socialising with contacts *is essential in building a rapport before negotiations begin.*
   means that I spend less time with my family.

Ask students how easy it would be for them to adjust their existing values or even completely accept any of the 'new' values. Which values could/n't they accept? Why?

Possible responses and information:

Values often form the basis of a culture, and are so deeply rooted that most people find it impossible to 'adopt' new values. This is worth bearing in mind when confronted with people whose values contrast sharply with your own.

If different cultures can't agree on values, how can we get along?

Try to unpack your own assumptions and 'cultural baggage'.

Respect and embrace the differences you observe.

Try to understand <u>why</u> people hold certain values.

Make an effort to learn about your contact's culture. (Get in touch with your embassy in a country before going there, look on the Internet for culture tips and advice.)

Observe and learn from the behaviour of your foreign contact(s).

Adapt your own communication style and behaviour when dealing with other cultures.

1.1 Team A Leadership

charismatic	inspiring	visionary	authoritarian	intimidating
unable to delegate	constructive criticism	goal setting	competent	task-focused
performance-related	management by results		procrastination	
get your hands dirty				

1.1 Team B Dream teams

team-bonding	performance review	team spirit	positive feedback
a huge asset	reliable and efficient	to gel as a team	commitment
communication	time management	conflict avoidance	to get on well with
breaking down barriers	morale		

108

Autocratic leadership

Our boss is like a dictator! If he (be) more democratic in the last few years, employee turnover wouldn't have been so high. He should (give) us some opportunities to make suggestions and contribute ideas.

Bureaucratic leadership

If we didn't always have to do everything 'by the book', we (can come up with) more creative business solutions. We're in a very competitive business sector and our director (should allow) more flexibility.

Charismatic leadership

I don't know what would happen if our CEO (leave) the company. We totally rely on his enthusiasm and energy to drive the business. Perhaps he should (encourage) the team to develop their skills a bit more in the future.

Democratic leadership

Our annual employee satisfaction surveys show that encouraging team members to contribute to the decision-making process has developed their skills and increased their motivation. If they (not have) this opportunity they might be more concerned about pay rises.

1.2

✂

Laissez-faire leadership

✂

Our team is highly experienced and we're generally just left to 'get on with it'. Our boss (not have) to be looking over our shoulders all the time. So, if she (need to bring) up to date on a project, we give her a project progress presentation.

✂

People-oriented leadership

✂

Our last project manager was just like one of the team. If he (not be) so supportive of our work and focused on developing us both as individuals and as a team, I don't think we would have achieved such a strong creative collaboration. We really should (nominate) him for the 'boss of the year' award before he retired.

✂

Task-oriented leadership

✂

Our boss only ever focuses on targets and 'getting the job done'. If she (not be) constantly checking up on us, she might have more time to focus on the welfare and motivation of our team. She should (be careful) as she's having difficulties in retaining staff.

✂

Transformational leadership

✂

Our president inspires her team constantly with a shared vision of the future. She's always available to talk to her employees and joins in a lot of meetings between junior staff. If she left the company, we (be) unlikely to get another president like her. However she does have to (support) by a lot of 'details people'.

✂

110

1.3

✂- -

Your country: Bravadia

Your culture: High-Power Distance / Masculine Culture / Low-Context

Your company: The Internet giant 'E-xplore'

Task 1: Elect a team leader

Task 2: Hold a meeting to decide how to deal with the following dilemma.

For political reasons, the Nasterian government is demanding that 'E-xplore' launches a new Internet search service in Nasteria that will limit what users there can access. At the same time, 'E-xplore' has been highly praised and globally recognised for its resistance to the Republic of Thimas government's efforts to obtain data on its users' search habits.

What should 'E-xplore' do? If it doesn't give in to the Nasterian government, it will lose its most significant market. If it does, it will compromise the integrity it has become famous for.

Note: Behave in accordance with Bravadian cultural values and attitudes.

✂- -

Your country: Placidia

Your culture: Low-Power Distance / Feminine Culture / High-Context

Your company: The Internet giant 'E-xplore'

Task 1: Elect a team leader

Task 2: Hold a meeting to decide how to deal with the following dilemma.

For political reasons, the Nasterian government is demanding that 'E-xplore' launches a new Internet search service in Nasteria that will limit what users there can access. At the same time, 'E-xplore' has been highly praised and globally recognised for its resistance to the Republic of Thimas government's efforts to obtain data on its users' search habits.

What should 'E-xplore' do? If it doesn't give in to the Nasterian government, it will lose its most significant market. If it does, it will compromise the integrity it has become famous for.

Note: Behave in accordance with Placidian cultural values and attitudes.

✂- -

1.3

Your country: Tacitalia

Your culture: High-Power Distance / Feminine Culture / High-Context

Your company: The Internet giant 'E-xplore'

Task 1: Elect a team leader

Task 2: Hold a meeting to decide how to deal with the following dilemma.

For political reasons, the Nasterian government is demanding that 'E-xplore' launches a new Internet search service in Nasteria that will limit what users there can access. At the same time, 'E-xplore' has been highly praised and globally recognised for its resistance to the Republic of Thimas government's efforts to obtain data on its users' search habits.

What should 'E-xplore' do? If it doesn't give in to the Nasterian government, it will lose its most significant market. If it does, it will compromise the integrity it has become famous for.

Note: Behave in accordance with Tacitalian cultural values and attitudes.

Your country: Bluntlund

Your culture: Low-Power Distance / Masculine Culture / Low-Context

Your company: The Internet giant 'E-xplore'

Task 1: Elect a team leader

Task 2: Hold a meeting to decide how to deal with the following dilemma.

For political reasons, the Nasterian government is demanding that 'E-xplore' launches a new Internet search service in Nasteria that will limit what users there can access. At the same time, 'E-xplore' has been highly praised and globally recognised for its resistance to the Republic of Thimas government's efforts to obtain data on its users' search habits.

What should 'E-xplore' do? If it doesn't give in to the Nasterian government, it will lose its most significant market. If it does, it will compromise the integrity it has become famous for.

Note: Behave in accordance with Bluntlundic cultural values and attitudes.

2.1 Student A (The architect)

- You are an architect and you are meeting a very important client for the first time at his/her office. You have already spoken several times on the telephone.
- Avoid making small talk because you want to discuss the items on the agenda.
- **For you, the AIM of the meeting is to discuss the points on the agenda below and ensure that the project will be on schedule.**

The agenda

1) The designs for the main structure

- Find out if the client has looked at the designs for the main structure and if he/she is satisfied with them.
- You would like his/her formal approval of the designs today so that you can begin work on the next stage tomorrow.

2) Interior layout

- Explain that placing the main staircase away from the entrance, as the client wished, is against fire safety regulations. The main staircase is an important escape route and it must lead directly to an exit.
- Inform the client that, fortunately, this is the only problem with the internal designs so there is no need to waste much time on further changes.
- Discourage your client from making any further changes. You do not want to get behind schedule.

Note:
You are keen to keep this project on schedule both for the client's sake and for your own reputation.

You have 6 minutes maximum for the whole meeting. You will miss your plane home if you overrun!

✂ -

2.1 Student B (The client)

- You are having a state-of-the-art building designed for your new offices. Today, the architect is coming to meet you for the first time. You have already spoken several times on the telephone.
- You would like to get to know your visitor before discussing the project, so make small talk for five minutes. Ask him/her about his/her journey / career / family / interests outside work, etc. Tell him/her a bit about yourself and your business.
- **For you, the AIM of the meeting is to get to know the architect.** Discussing the points on the agenda is not a priority but, if you do have time to look at it, go straight to point 2 as you are very concerned about this.

The agenda

1) The designs for the main structure

- You have seen the designs for the main structure and you are very happy with them.
- However, before you give formal approval, you would like to show them to your colleague when you go to New York next week.

2) Interior layout

- Last week, the architect said that building the main staircase away from the entrance may be against fire safety regulations. Ask whether he/she has found out if this is the case.
- Explain that you would like to move the reception and visitors' centre from the *left* side of the entrance to the *right*.

Note:
You have a lot of things to do today. During the meeting:
leave the room for one minute to speak to your secretary about

- an urgent issue
- a one-minute call from a colleague who is offering to meet you at the airport next week.

You have 10 minutes for the meeting but it doesn't matter if you overrun by a few minutes.

2.1 The observer

Observe a meeting between an architect and his/her client.

As you watch, take notes on the following points:

1) Small talk

   Who initiated the small talk?

   How many minutes were spent on this?

2) Business / The agenda

   How many minutes were spent on this?

   Who seemed more focused on the agenda?

3) Schedules / Deadlines

   Did they discuss schedules / deadlines? What was the outcome?

4) Distractions / Interruptions

   What distractions or interruptions took place?

   Do both people seem comfortable with these events?

5) Feelings

   Do you think they are both satisfied with the meeting?
   Why? Why not?